DEPARTMENT OF THE NAVY
HEADQUARTERS UNITED STATES MARINE CORPS
WASHINGTON, D.C. 20380-1775

4 March 2014

FOREWORD

The past decade makes clear that responsiveness and versatility – the institutional trademarks of the Marine Corps – are always in demand. Even as we took the fight to the enemy in Iraq and Afghanistan, U.S. Marines were the "first responders" to the tsunamis in the Indian Ocean and Japan, earthquakes in Pakistan and Haiti and the typhoon in the Philippines. As the Nation's Expeditionary Force in Readiness, we are and will continue to be heavily engaged around the world.

While meeting current commitments and preserving readiness, the Marine Corps must reconfigure and refit to meet coming challenges. The future evolving and complex security environment will only increase the demands on the Marine Corps. The law requires and our heritage demands that we maintain a force that is naval in character and capable of conducting amphibious operations. The Geographic Combatant Commanders need us to give them the three-fold advantages of forward presence: the recurring dividends of "soft power" applied with a richer military dimension; the deterrent effect of immediate, credible and effective actions to thwart potential adversaries; and the expanded operational reach and tactical flexibility to defeat foes throughout the littorals. The American people will surely continue to expect – and the world will count on – Marines to be the leading edge of humanitarian relief and disaster recovery operations.

Expeditionary Force 21 is our vision for designing and developing the force that will continue to fulfill these responsibilities. But it is more than a vision – it is also an actionable plan and a disciplined process to shape and guide our capability and capacity decisions while respecting our country's very real need to regain budgetary discipline. True to our expeditionary ethos, we will work with a clear-eyed view of what will be asked of us and seek only what we believe is necessary. Nimble by organizational design and adaptive by culture, we will rely on open-mindedness and creativity and make the best of what we have. Through Expeditionary Force 21 we will chart a course over the next 10 years to field a Marine Corps that will be: ***the right force in the right place at the right time***.

Semper Fidelis,

James E. Amos
General, U.S. Marine Corps
Commandant of the Marine Corps

Expeditionary Force 21 Capstone Concept
Table of Contents

> **"The Marine Corps' inherent agility, crisis response capabilities, and maritime focus make it well suited to carry out many priority missions under the President's defense strategy."**
>
> **—Chuck Hagel, Secretary of Defense**

I. Expeditionary Force 21 Context

Expeditionary Force 21 provides guidance for how the Marine Corps Total Force—as an integral part of the larger naval and joint team—will be postured, organized, trained, and equipped to fulfill assigned public law and national policy responsibilities.[1] Expeditionary Force 21 does not change *what* Marines do, but *how* they will do it. Expeditionary Force 21 draws guidance from national security direction and naval strategy as described by *A Cooperative Strategy for 21st Century Seapower*. Expeditionary Force 21 will be integrated with the Marine Corps Service Campaign Plan 2014-2022 and Marine Corps Strategic Health Assessment.

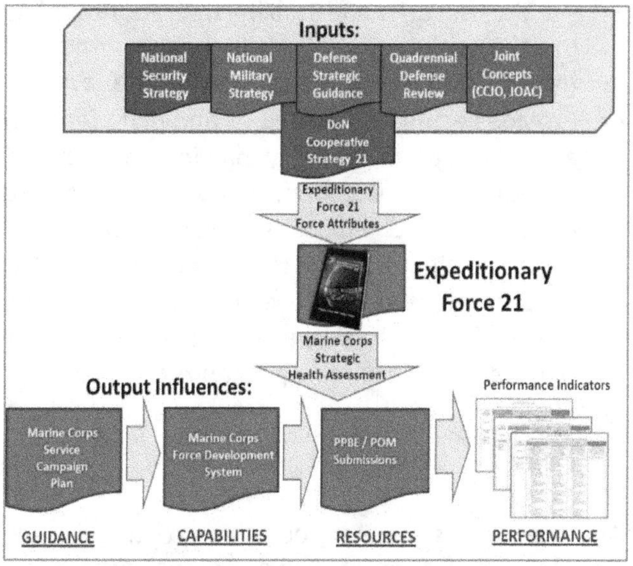

MCDP 1-0 Operations, Aug 2011, provided an operational and doctrinal foundation that incorporated proven concepts such as Operational Maneuver From the Sea, Ship to Objective Maneuver, Seabasing and Marine Corps Operating Concepts (MOC). Expeditionary Force 21 builds on that "now" doctrinal foundation by providing guidance for concepts and capabilities while informing our force posture, organization, and capabilities over a 10-year period.

Expeditionary Force 21 is our new capstone concept replacing the Marine Corps Vision and Strategy 2025 and will align future concepts, advocate plans, and capability roadmaps. We will annually assess capabilities, priorities, long range vision and future operating environment to inform annual updates to Expeditionary Force 21.

Figure 1: Expeditionary Force 21 aligns capability development with strategic guidance

Expeditionary Force 21 provides an aspirational vision of how we will operate in order to guide experimentation, force development activities, and inform programming decisions. Some goals within Expeditionary Force 21 will be achieved quickly while others will require continued work and coordination to develop. However, the overarching goal is to improve how we support the requirements of Geographic Combatant Commanders (GCCs) by providing *the right force in the right place at the right time*.

---

[1] Recognizing the need for and benefit of, expeditionary responsiveness and operational versatility, the 82nd Congress (through the Douglas-Mansfield Act) codified that the Marine Corps provides the Nation an expeditionary force in readiness. This mandate has since been incorporated and expanded upon within the United States Code, Title 10, and Department of Defense Directive 5100.01, *Functions of the Department of Defense and Its Major Components*.

II. Role of the Marine Corps

The Marine Corps is a naval, expeditionary force-in-readiness tasked in public law and national policy to perform the following specific functions:

- Seize and defend advanced naval bases or lodgments to facilitate subsequent joint operations.
- Provide close air support for ground forces.
- Conduct land and air operations essential to the prosecution of a naval campaign.
- Conduct expeditionary operations in the urban littorals and other challenging environments.
- Conduct amphibious operations, including engagement, crisis response, and power projection operations, to assure access. ***The Marine Corps has primary responsibility for the development of amphibious doctrine, tactics, techniques, and equipment***.
- Conduct security and stability operations and assist the initial establishment of a military government, pending transfer of this responsibility to another authority.
- Provide security detachments and units for service on armed vessels of the Navy, provide protection of naval property at naval stations and bases, and provide security at designated US embassies and consulates.
- Perform other duties as the President or the Secretary of Defense may direct. These additional duties may not detract from or interfere with the operations for which the Marine Corps is primarily organized.

Figure 2: Marine Corps Role

III. What "Being Expeditionary" Means to Marines

An expedition is a military operation conducted by an armed force to accomplish a specific objective in a foreign country. The U.S. Armed Forces participate in expeditions, with each contributing complementary capabilities: Navy, Air Force, and Army are optimized to dominate the sea, air, and land, respectively while the Coast Guard is optimized to safeguard our maritime interests. While the Marine Corps may operate on and from the sea, in and from the air, and on the land, it is not optimized to dominate any domain. Rather, the Marine Corps is optimized to be ***expeditionary*** — a strategically mobile force that is light enough to get to the crisis quickly, yet able to accomplish the mission or provide time and options prior to the arrival of additional forces.

To Marines, being expeditionary includes an institutional ethos and predisposition that influences every aspect of organization, training, and equipment. It connotes more than the mere ability to deploy overseas when needed. It is an institutional imperative that acknowledges the necessity to deploy rapidly, arrive quickly, and begin operating immediately. This expeditionary ethos is the most critical contributor to the Corps' success in crisis response and complex contingencies. This ethos has been deliberately cultivated and exploited by Marine leaders for generations. It is this mind-set that drives our capability development efforts and ultimately generates both combat power and the organizational flexibility to accomplish diverse missions across the range of military operations (ROMO). Our expeditionary culture can be summarized simply: ***fast***, ***austere***, and ***lethal***.

Figure 3: "Fast Austere & Lethal"

The expeditionary mind-set is not dependent on acquisition. It is instead derived from discipline, training, and an overwhelming need to accomplish the mission regardless of the situation. An expeditionary force is built on several key principles:

- Solving problems with minimal support and broad guidance.
- Deploying and employing tailored, economical forces of almost any size and configuration.
- Deploying where there is no infrastructure and operating immediately.
- Achieving success in those missions where action delayed is action denied.
- Living and operating in austere conditions where large support bases are unacceptable or infeasible.
- Minimizing potential adverse cultural and political impact by stepping lightly in all areas of support and infrastructure and working with our regional partners to achieve success.
- Working with affected populations wherever deployed—because we respect and protect those who are caught in the middle of a conflict or disaster.
- Maintaining equipment, including aviation, in forward areas with organic assets.
- Enhancing partnerships with Special Operations Forces that exploit our complementary capabilities.

> "What are expeditionary forces? They are power projection forces, but they are much more. Power projection is part of an expeditionary force, included in the 'sticker price.' An expeditionary force is like the expeditionary warriors that man it. They have an expeditionary state of mind; they are comfortable with uncertainty and capable of handling adversity; they have the ability to adapt 'out there' and to improvise; they have the ability to start from scratch and make up solutions as they go; they have the ability to do it with less—to drive a nail with a shovel if they don't have a hammer."
>
> —General Charles E. Wilhelm, USMC, Expeditionary Warfare, 1995

IV. Expeditionary Force 21 Attributes

Expeditionary Force In "Readiness"
- 1/3 of operating forces deployed forward for deterrence and proximity to crises
- Self-sustaining under austere conditions

Middleweight Force
- Light enough for rapid response
- Heavy enough to prevail in the littorals

Modern Force
- Preserves quantitative edge over opponents
- Exploits innovative concepts and approaches

Integrated Combined Arms Force
- Applies all aspects of joint combat power
- Extends power of naval forces

Integrated Naval Force
- Command and control exploits the sea as maneuver space
- Leverages traditional and innovative operating concepts

Force Biased for Action
- Poised for rapid crisis response – no tiered readiness
- Readily Deployable-Employable-Sustainable forces

Leading Edge of Joint Force
- Regionally oriented MEFs and MEBs
- Small fly-in command element capable of transitioning to a joint warfighting headquarters

Forcible Entry In Depth
- Scalable to crisis, contingency or forcible entry
- Capable of projecting two MEBs from the sea
- Seizes and holds for follow-on joint forces

Figure 4 –Eight Attributes underpin the Expeditionary Force 21 design

As an Expeditionary Force in Readiness, the Marine Corps' main missions are "the ability to respond to crisis" and "assure littoral access[2]." Given this emphasis our focus ranges from security cooperation to forcible entry with a special emphasis on crisis response. Fulfilling this role requires a forward posture with the right capabilities to deploy, employ, and sustain our forces in expeditionary and austere environments. Forward stationing and forward deployed forces requires developing a force structure that meets steady-state activities at a 1:2 dwell for the Active Component and 1:4 dwell for the Reserve Component along with a high degree of readiness. Additionally we intend to examine and enhance our role within the Global Response Force (GRF) by providing multiple force and headquarter options. Expeditionary Force 21 is designed to focus the Marine Corps on meeting the nation's crisis response

---

[2] Marine Corps Operating Concepts, 2010.

needs by having a readily deployable, employable, and sustainable power projection force tailored to meet the GCC's operational needs from steady-state activities to forcible entry. Fully realizing these attributes holds many implications for Marine Corps planning and prioritization.

V. Future Operating Environment

The future operating environment will continue to be characterized by national and international challenges that will stretch the employment capacity of the U.S. military and demand a force in readiness with capabilities for a global response. We must expect a security landscape characterized by volatility, instability and complexity. The proliferation of modern conventional and cyberspace weapons to a broader range of state and non-state entities, along with the erosion of U.S. technological advantages in areas where we have long enjoyed relative superiority, is likely to continue. We must account for a growing potential among adversaries to employ weapons of mass destruction. Further, the actions of transnational criminal organizations and violent extremist groups will contribute to regional unrest and instability that directly threaten U.S. interests through piracy, trafficking and terrorism. Advances in information technology and cyberspace capabilities create both opportunities and challenges. As global connectivity and social media increase awareness of human suffering in the wake of disasters, we will surely see a continuation of the recent trend towards applying military capabilities for humanitarian assistance and disaster relief. However, this global connectivity can also amplify the inevitable frictions that stem from logistical missteps and cultural misunderstandings between assisting forces and local populations.

The majority of these challenges and opportunities will be in the congested and diverse areas where the sea and land merge—the littorals. Most maritime activities—commercial shipping, fishing, and oil and gas extraction, for example—take place within 200 miles of the shore. Additionally, more than 80 percent of the world's population currently resides within 100 miles of a coastline—and the proportion is increasing. In many cases threats to our interests may require expanding the concept of littoral maneuver to hundreds of miles inland to resolve crises. As such, geography and demographics point towards a future security environment with a significant littoral dimension. It is no accident that the so-called "Arc of Instability" encompasses the littoral areas of South Central Asia, the Middle East, Africa and Central and South America.

The readiness, rapid responsiveness, flexibility, precision and strategic mobility of naval forces are essential to ensuring continued access and security in the global commons and the littoral regions that border them. While the need to conduct sustained operations ashore should never be ruled out, it is more likely that the next 10 years will be largely characterized by the need to address small-scale crises and limited contingencies in and around the littorals. Should major operations and campaigns occur, they are increasingly certain to involve significant combat in the maritime domain and the littorals.

The increased likelihood of operations in the littorals requires a renewed focus on the Marine Corps' Title 10 responsibility to be organized, trained and equipped, "for service with the fleet in the seizure and defense of advanced naval bases." While this task appeared anachronistic to some during much of the Cold War and the years immediately thereafter, it is taking on renewed importance in this emerging security environment. Conflicting claims over portions of the sea and its resources, growing naval competition, and the rise in land-based threats to access are all indicators that future joint campaigns are more likely to be naval in character. The development and proliferation of anti-access and area-denial (A2/AD) capabilities threaten freedom of action at sea and endanger the limited number of U.S.

bases overseas. These conditions are remarkably similar to those that existed before and during World War II in the Pacific, but with the added challenge of the increased range and precision of modern sensors and weapons. During that conflict, the ability to establish advanced bases and deny an adversary the use of his bases played a key role in gaining and maintaining air and maritime superiority.

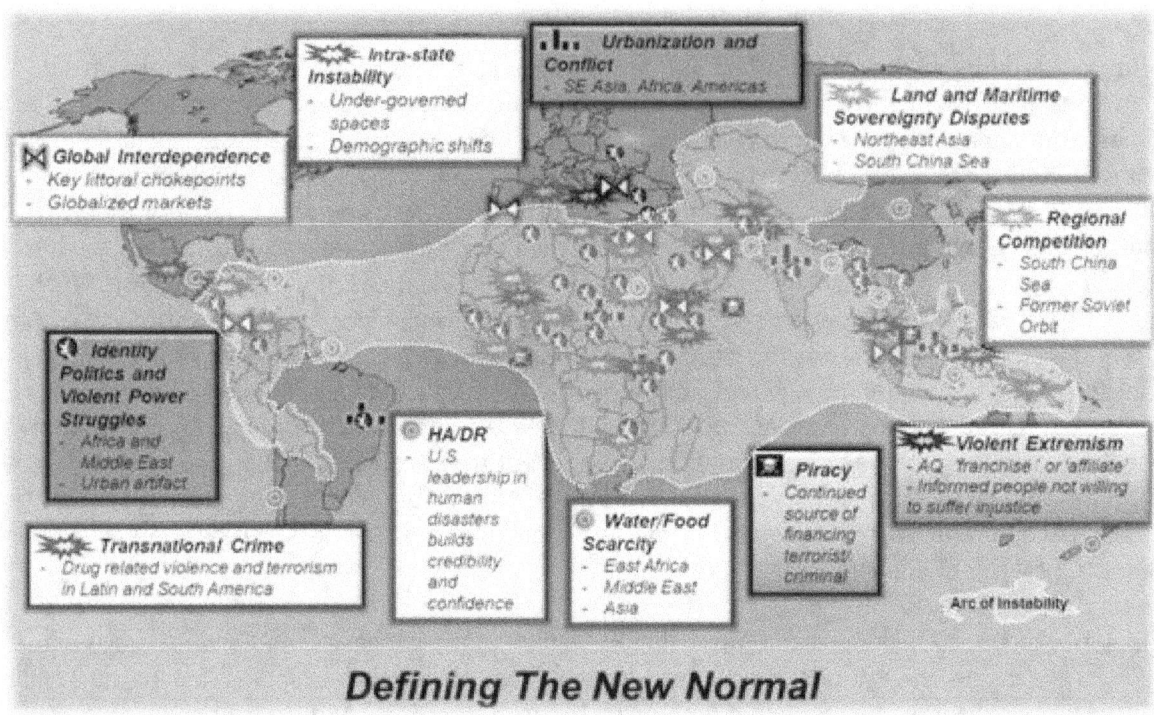

Figure 5: Areas of Instability Overlap with Key Littoral Areas

The solution to today's problem requires the ability to fight across all domains in a holistic, coordinated manner along with the ability to project power and control the sea. Similarly, establishing and operating from advanced austere bases remains a key operational capability. While a number of initiatives are underway to improve the coordinated application of air, sea, and cyberspace capabilities, landward considerations have not been adequately addressed thus far. The *Joint Operational Access Concept* acknowledges that "maintaining and expanding operational access may require entry of land forces into hostile territory for a number of reasons. These may range from limited-objective attacks, such as raids to eliminate land-based threats to friendly air and naval forces, to seizing a lodgment for a sustained land campaign."

The ability to use the sea and advanced bases to "turn the A2/AD table" on an adversary, either prior to or in the midst of a conflict, has not been fully considered by concept developers and policy-makers. Similarly, the ability to establish a network of numerous austere advanced bases—by occupation or seizure—as a means of dispersing aircraft, missiles, and intelligence, surveillance, and reconnaissance assets needs to be comprehensively explored. Establishing—or merely demonstrating the ability to rapidly establish—such "oceanic outposts" would strengthen our ability to reassure allies and deter adversaries.

The increased range, precision, and proliferation of A2/AD systems highlight the need to conduct dispersed operations with smaller, task-organized forces. There are other reasons to operate in this way. The GCCs are increasing their demand for tailored forces to conduct theater security cooperation activities with a wider number of partner nations. Ranging from security force assistance to combined training exercises, Phase 0 activities are important elements of both a service's engagement strategy and the GCC's Theater Security Cooperation Plan. These activities ensure access prior to the start of contingencies and contribute directly to the reduction of ungoverned spaces from which future adversaries may originate. Notwithstanding, theater commanders must still be prepared to quickly consolidate and reorganize forces into larger formations to expeditiously deal with escalating crises and contingencies. These competing demands call for a new approach to how we organize, deploy and employ forces—especially with regard to effectively linking Marine Corps, Navy, Coast Guard, Special Operations Command and partner capabilities. This starts with revising our approach to capability and capacity development.

As the Nation prepares for an uncertain future, the Naval Services provide essential capabilities to deter conflict, build alliances, deny sanctuary, enable influence and, when required, project power against increasingly lethal and asymmetric adversaries. Rapidly evolving security and fiscal concerns demand changes in our forward-deployed, crisis response force to include new operational thinking, concepts, capabilities, and partnerships.

VI. Our Approach

For several decades, the Marine Corps' capability and capacity development efforts were focused on enhancing the ability of our largest type of Marine air-ground task force (MAGTF),[3] the Marine Expeditionary Force (MEF),[4] to conduct major operations and campaigns. The ability to conduct security cooperation activities and crisis response was generally derived from capabilities designed for major combat operations. However, the current and projected security environment requires a reshaping of the force to meet the growing demand for security cooperation activities and a focus on crisis response without forfeiting our ability to fight as a significant force in any large conflict or enduring war. Building on the proven concepts of Operational Maneuver From the Sea, Ship to Objective Maneuver, and Seabasing, Expeditionary Force 21 expands the scope and capabilities of these concepts to meet the operating environment challenges of today and tomorrow. Accordingly, we will adjust our focus to achieve the required capabilities and capacities to become *the right force in the right place at the right time*.

Figure 6: Expeditionary Force 21---
Crisis Response

---

[3] Marine Corps forces are normally task-organized for operations by forming MAGTFs—balanced; air-ground, combined arms formations under a single commander. Each MAGTF is composed of a command element (CE), a ground combat element (GCE), an aviation combat element (ACE), and logistics combat element (LCE).

[4] The MEFs are the principal warfighting organizations of the Marine Corps, capable of conducting and sustaining expeditionary operations in any geographic environment. The current standing MEFs vary somewhat in size, with the largest being approximately 40,000 Marines and Sailors. In addition to their warfighting role, MEFs task-organize subordinate units into smaller MAGTFs or other formations to support the Geographic Combatant Commanders' requirements.

Expeditionary Force 21

For the Marine Corps to remain effective as the nation's forward-engaged and ready for crisis force, we must align how we operate with the conditions imposed by the evolving security environment. These conditions will pose challenges that the Marine Corps will meet by providing conventional deterrence, conducting proactive engagement, and performing crisis response as part of a larger naval force. As explained in *A Cooperative Strategy for 21st Century Seapower*, the common denominator of our future success is improving our stance as a ***forward, ready and flexible*** expeditionary element of the naval team. With a greater proportion of the force forward over a wider area, we will continue to provide time and options for our Nation's leaders to assess, decide and respond to concerns and problems around the globe. Naval forces operating from the sea and from austere forward bases can adjust their activities and visibility to suit the dynamic political conditions associated with crises. A forward-deployed force that can immediately shift from security cooperation activities to crisis response and combat operations is a Marine Corps specific resource both diplomatically and militarily, providing assurance to partners and insurance for our Nation.

The intent of Expeditionary Force 21 is to maximize our ability to meet the coming challenges. Accordingly, our approach to capability and capacity development is being redirected to:

- Increase forward presence with a posture that ensures one-third of the active operating forces are immediately available for employment. This is intended to develop partnerships, enhance awareness, deter adversaries, expand GCC options, and improve response times when actions are required.
- Regionally orient, resource, and employ Marine Corps operating forces to ensure familiarity between GCC and Marine Corps commanders and staffs. Regional orientation is intended to promote consistency in operations and procedures among naval forces, special operations forces (SOF), partners and the interagency communities.
- Inform crisis response and contingency planning with current and relevant local knowledge gained from steady-state activities with partner nations, naval components, and SOF.
- To maintain consistency of operational command, establish standing headquarters that can:
    - Rapidly deploy fly-in command elements to form and fight scalable MAGTFs during a crisis.
    - Seamlessly expand to control a larger combined joint task force (CJTF).
    - Support an already established JTF.
- Provide timely and scalable forces for crisis response, allowing commanders to tailor force footprints to evolving situations and effectively composite modular MAGTFs by combining forward-deployed forces with rapidly deploying forces.
- Improve our ability to operate effectively in task-organized, distributed formations to counter growing threats from proliferating technologies that improve an enemy's capabilities.
- Improve the capability to train, organize and equip the MAGTF to operate and succeed in an operational environment where WMD is present or CWMD is the primary mission of the MAGTF.
- Improve our ability to shape the operating environment and, if required, conduct forcible entry operations as a service or as part of a joint force.
- Prosecute complex combat operations throughout the littorals as part of an integrated naval force that entails:
    - Marine Corps integration into the Maritime Operations Centers.
    - Alternative seabased platforms for basing and theater security cooperation.
    - Alternative platforms for aggregating the MAGTF and responding to crisis.
    - Effective operational and tactical maneuver in the littorals that gains and retains the initiative.
    - Extended or indefinite sustainment from the sea through improved logistics relationships with naval forces and forward installations.

- Enhance our ability to operate in an increasingly complex environment characterized by the growth of social media, availability of information technology, importance of signature management, challenges to electromagnetic spectrum (EMS) access, and the globalization of cyberspace capabilities.
- Increase collaboration with SOF and further develop Marine Corps reconnaissance capability and capacity to ensure the ability to integrate operations, prepare the environment, and identify and defeat threats.

VII. Lines of Effort

Our capability development efforts and capacity decisions will be pursued along four intertwined lines of effort:

1. Refining Our Organization

Organization frames all the elements of force development. The MAGTF, owing to its proven flexibility, will remain our primary construct for organizing forces for missions across the ROMO. That said, we will explore and experiment with organizational refinements to improve our ability to **command and control, deploy, employ, and sustain** Marine Corps forces. This includes regional orientations that enhance habitual relationships but do not preclude forces from being available to support requirements on a global scale. These changes include:

- **Marine Expeditionary Force (MEF).** The MEFs provide the structure and capabilities that comprise the largest groupings of Marine Corps operating forces. MEF command elements will continue to enable large-scale Marine Corps participation in major joint operations. The MEF (Fwd) provides an additional command element option for the MEF. The value of this command element was proven in Operation Enduring Freedom and Operation Iraqi Freedom over the last decade. The MEF will be employed when it is required to meet the dynamics of a combined/joint operating environment. The overall MEF posture will evolve from three to two operational standing MEF CEs which are sufficient to support the national strategy and how we intend to operate.

  As defined by U. S. Code, Title 10, Chapter 507, Section 5063, "...the Marine Corps, within the Department of the Navy, shall be so organized as to include not less than three combat divisions and three air wings, and such other land combat, aviation, and other services as may be organic therein." In accordance with the mandate of the law, each MEF includes a command element with a MEF headquarters group, a ground combat element (GCE) with one Marine Division, an aviation combat element (ACE) with one Marine Aircraft Wing, and a logistics combat element (LCE) with one Marine Logistics Group. When employed the MEF may include more than one division, wing, or Marine Logistics Group. I MEF, based in Camp Pendleton, California, will focus on maintaining proficiency in major operations and campaigns as well as requirements associated with the Global Response Force (GRF) responsibilities. III MEF, based in Okinawa, Japan, will remain regionally oriented on the full range of military operations within that theater, to include designation as a standing joint task force headquarters for U.S. Pacific Command (PACOM) capable of combined operations. II MEF will merge with MARFORCOM HQ in

> **The MEF has the structure, equipment and capacity to streamline command and control of a long-term operation, providing the stability, continuity, economy, and long-range planning that are vital to success.**

Norfolk, VA, and the new MARFORCOM/II MEF HQ will command 2D MARDIV, 2D MAW, 2D MLG, and 2D MEB.

- **Marine Expeditionary Brigades (MEBs).** As our main effort in force development, the MEB will conduct planning and exercise command and control (C2) of forces conducting steady-state activities, responding to crises or contingencies, and forcible entry operations. The MEB will be organized and equipped to exercise command and control of joint and multi-national task forces, enable the MEF for larger JTF operations, or integrate with the Navy for the conduct of amphibious operations. MEB development will

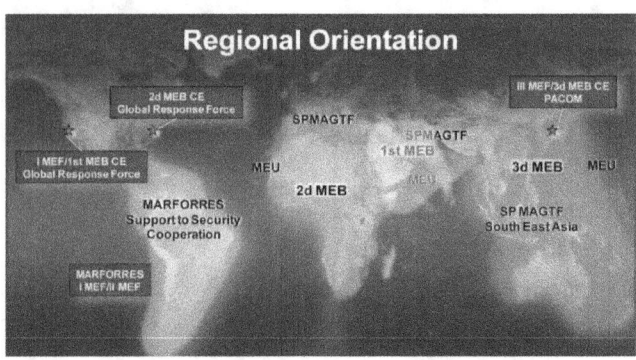

Figure 7:   Regional Orientation

include establishing JTF-capable MEB CEs that are regionally focused to meet GCCs needs. Another characteristic is the ability to composite forward and merge rapidly deploying Marine Corps forces into a cohesive, agile force scaled to the mission. This will make the MEBs the centerpiece of an expeditionary force in readiness prepared for immediate, effective employment in any type of crisis or conflict.

I MEF has a global response focus and is oriented on PACOM and U.S. Central Command (CENTCOM), 1st MEB will orient on the CENTCOM Area of Responsibility (AOR) and will support GRF requirements. At Camp Lejeune, North Carolina, the standing 2d MEB CE will regionally orient on U.S. Africa Command (AFRICOM) and U.S. European Command (EUCOM) and also support the GRF. Established under III MEF, 3d MEB is a standing command element regionally oriented on PACOM. Additionally, MARCENT, the Marine component within CENTCOM, is capable of integrating with the NAVCENT component as part of an integrated naval command operating as a forward operational command element. The development of the MEB, as articulated in the MEB concept of operations, will include light, medium and heavy options to provide a scalable and responsive force capable of executing operations across the ROMO in support of GCC requirements (see Figure 7).

- **Marine Expeditionary Units (MEUs).** The MEUs and their associated Amphibious Ready Groups (ARGs) will continue to provide forward presence in key regions through a combination of forward basing and rotational deployments. The MEU's strength is its ability to respond to crises as an integrated MAGTF. During the next 10 years, we must explore evolving the MEU to accommodate changes in basing, capability, capacity, as well as exploration of, prepositioned equipment, land basing, complementary force packages, and alternative platforms. The MEUs may operate in a disaggregated or split manner.[5] While not optimal, they will be resourced to mitigate the risk when operating in this manner. This will include appropriate command and control assets and arrangements to accomplish a wider range of steady-state security activities as well as provide an immediate response to emergencies and episodic crises. When required, MEUs will composite with other forward forces to provide the foundation of a MEB or perform contingency operations.

---

[5] Split operations require elements of the ARG/MEU to function separately for various durations and various distances with the ARG and MEU commanders retaining control of forces under the same GCC.

Disaggregated operations require elements of the ARG/MEU to function separately and independently, regardless of time and distance, with elements under a command relationship that changes/limits the ARG and MEU commanders' control of their forces. The ARG/MEU may be disaggregated within a GCC's area of responsibility (AOR) or elements of the ARG/MEU may be attached to a different GCC.

- **Special Purpose MAGTFs (SPMAGTFs).**[6] SPMAGTFs will assume a greater role in crisis response and generate greater capacity for forward presence in more locations. Based on GCC requirements, these organizations are tailored appropriately to conduct security cooperation activities with partner nations in order to develop interoperability, facilitate access, build defense and security relationships, gain regional understanding, and position for immediate response to episodic crises.

- **Global Response Force.** Each CONUS-based MEF provides a MEU to the GRF. Within the upcoming year we will examine the feasibility of increasing force options and including a MEB JTF-capable command element in the GRF. In addition to or as part of our GRF commitment, each MEF provides Alert Contingency MAGTFs for immediate employment in response to crisis. These forces are ready for employment within hours of notification and are central to our crisis response and compositing concepts. These forces can leverage prepositioned assets to provide sustained MAGTF response capabilities in key regions.

- **MARFORs.** Regional Marine Corps Forces Commands, as the Marine component within a GCC, support theater security cooperation activities as well as provide advice on Marine Corps' capabilities in order to set conditions for crisis and contingency response. Regional MARFORs provide the means in which forward-deployed units gain and maintain regional understanding and awareness, to include critical links with country teams, allies, host nations, and partner nations. Regional MARFORs additionally work with their Navy, Coast Guard, and Special Operations counterparts to inform and synchronize the planning and execution of integrated maritime security cooperation activities in support of GCC objectives. The regional MARFOR is the linchpin connecting forward deploying forces with the GCC. However, just as critical is manning within the GCC staff and supporting the GCC planning and coordination efforts.

- **Infantry Battalions and Company Landing Teams.** Infantry battalions will remain the Marine Corps' standard unit of deployment; however, company landing teams may take on a larger role in crisis response and may form the GCE component of a SPMAGTF. The tables of organization and equipment for the infantry battalion will be reviewed over the next few years in order to ensure that they have the capability and capacity to support one or more employed company landing teams simultaneously. Company landing teams provide a means to engage forward in more locations and respond to crises. During entry operations they enable dispersed operations to secure landing sites or maneuver deep to inland objectives. Lastly, they must have the maneuver capability to disperse and mass throughout the littorals. During crisis response they can form the basis of an immediate response.

- **MAGTF-SOF Integration.** Continued development of the integrated SOF Liaison Element will increase integration of our MEUs and SOF. Tactically, the Special Operation Forces Liaison Elements will help collaborate special operation efforts and conventional forces efforts to achieve overall mission success from both sides. Our goal is to expand this integration to all forward forces such as SPMAGTFs by developing a more deliberate path for MAGTF-SOF operational integration through joint concept development, experimentation and exercises with United States Special Operations Command (USSOCOM) through Marine Corps Forces Special Operations Command (MARSOC). This includes developing, experimenting with and exercising tactics, techniques, and procedures for the

---

[6] When situations arise for which a MEU or other unit is either inappropriate or unavailable, an SPMAGTF is formed. An SPMAGTF may be of any size —but normally no larger than a MEU—with tailored capabilities required to accomplish a particular mission.

incorporation of SOF preparation of the environment activities that support the introduction of expeditionary forces for crisis response and contingency operations. In addition, the same type of development efforts should be directed towards MAGTF-SOF integration with respect to remote collaborative planning and synchronization of operations under the supported/supporting relationship construct. In order to maximize opportunities with SOF, we will explore greater staff integration at the GCC level.

- **Expeditionary Advance Base Operations.** We are developing concepts to secure advanced expeditionary bases of operations as part of a naval campaign. Employing Marine Corps aircraft from multiple expeditionary advanced bases and amphibious warfare ships, as integrated elements of overall naval operations, complicates adversary targeting and increases our offensive options. Reinforcing expeditionary advanced bases with long-range strike, anti-ship, and anti-air systems can transform the capability into a sea denial outpost. These expeditionary sites can also serve as a base for offensive actions in support of sea control, such as strikes, raids, or seizure of additional advanced bases. Once secured, such bases would also provide additional hubs supporting the integrated naval logistics network. Securing multiple austere bases and airfields requires not only amphibious capabilities, but a host of expeditionary enablers (BEACHGRU, SEABEE, etc.) resident in the Navy Expeditionary Combat Command (NECC) as well as joint complementary capabilities. Establishing such "oceanic outposts" would require a modern-day capability similar to defense battalion organizations.[7] Theater security cooperation activities that account for establishing these expeditionary sites must be well-integrated and planned.

- **Manpower.** Policies and procedures must evolve to support global force management and commanders' requirements to maintain appropriate readiness levels across all structured and task-organized organizations inside and outside CONUS. It is essential to develop a total force (reserve and active forces) approach to supporting regional orientation and sourcing GCC requirements. In many instances our reserve forces provide an institutional shock absorber to meet expanding requirements for employing Marine forces in theater security cooperation and contingency response. Additionally, we must review sourcing and rotation for all MAGTF elements in coordination with the Navy.

2. Adjusting Our Forward Posture

Expeditionary Force 21 envisions a posture in which one-third of the Marine Corps' operating forces will be persistently positioned forward, with a greater variety of unit types distributed appropriately across areas of command responsibility. This gives each GCC the three-fold advantages of forward presence: the recurring dividends available from "soft power"; deterrence derived from credible and capable response; and the freedom of action created by expanded operational reach and tactical flexibility. The Marine Corps will continue the process of tailoring our forward presence. This will enhance our ability to conduct sustained security cooperation activities and develop and maintain interoperability with partner nations, facilitate access, promote stability, deter adversaries, enhance the security of global commerce, and respond to crises as directed by the GCCs. Maintaining a forward-deployed posture to meet crisis response requirements and conduct theater security cooperation activities will require a total force effort to maintain a sustainable 1:2 deployment-to-dwell ratio for active forces and the operational use

---

[7] *Advanced Bases in Micronesia*, Fleet Marine Force Reference Publication (FMFRP) 12-46, and WWII-era Defense Battalions.

of reserve forces with a deployment-to-dwell ratio of 1:4. This deployment-to-dwell ratio is dependent on a high degree of readiness and integration of our forward stationed and rotational forces. This will require alternative approaches to existing paradigms for assigning and allocating forces to the GCCs. Figure 8 below depicts our goals.

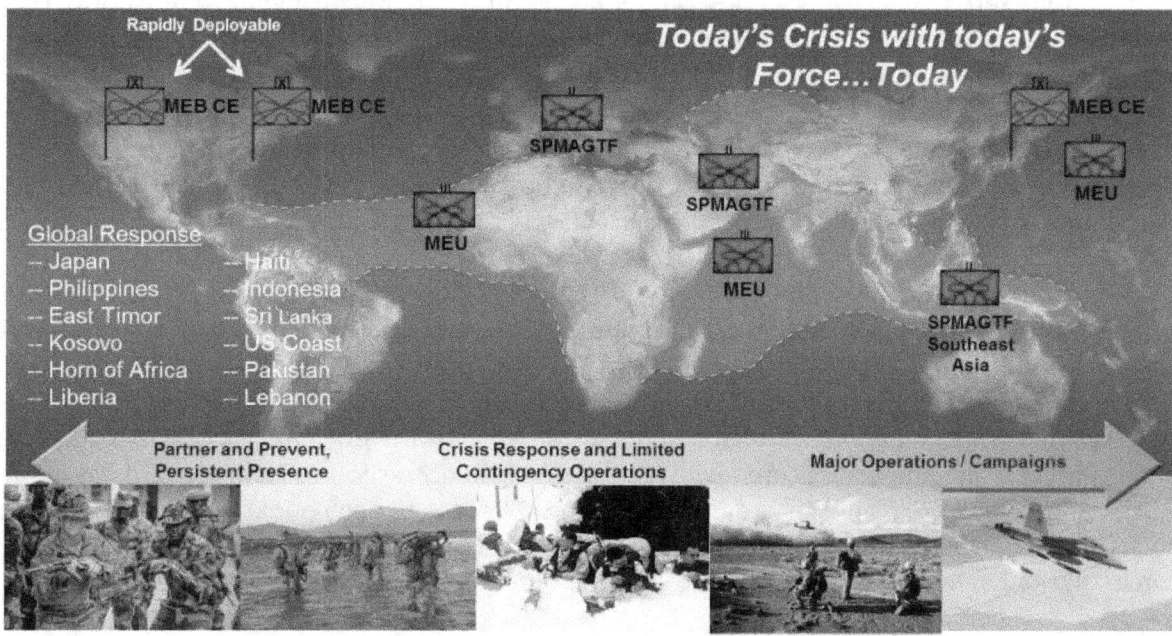

Figure 8: Poised for Response

For the **EUCOM/AFRICOM AORs**, the goal is a single seabased MAGTF trained for both aggregated and disaggregated employment. Subordinate task-organized forces will be employed in theater security cooperation activities while maintaining readiness for crisis response. Each disaggregated force may be embarked on single amphibious ships or exploit other combinations of shipping and/or basing ashore. When required this MAGTF can aggregate and composite with other forces in response to crises. The 2d MEB CE will be oriented on this region to support steady state activities and crisis response with three MAGTFs/MEUs in direct support.

- Within the **CENTCOM AOR** our goal is one rotational ARG/MEU tailored for crisis and contingency response with no less than 1.0 presence, and a SPMAGTF tailored for steady-state activities and crisis response. MARCENT coordinates employment of steady-state activities; however, 1st MEB CE will orient on this region for crisis response.

- The **PACOM AOR** will have a forward-based ARG/MEU augmented by additional 90-day seabased MAGTF patrols and transiting ARG/MEUs. Our goal is to source the forward-based MEU from the West Coast and employ one-year assignments to the MEU to enhance efficient use of assets. Additionally, units from I MEF, 2d MEB, MARFORCOM/II MEF, and Marine Corps Forces Reserve (MARFORRES) will rotationally deploy to PACOM where, as part of III MEF, they may conduct a variety of steady-state activities and support crisis response. To do so they may be task-organized under 3d MEB or SPMAGTFs and employed from amphibious ships, alternative shipping, or expeditionary locations ashore throughout Southeast Asia.

- The **SOUTHCOM AOR** will have rotational security cooperation teams fulfilling GCC theater security cooperation requirements. These organizations will be relatively small and focused on the maritime interdiction of transnational criminal organizational and security cooperation activities with regional partners. When required, SPMAGTFs may also be established in this AOR to conduct security cooperation exercises and events. MARFORRES will orient on this region and meet most GCC theater security cooperation requirements through training opportunities and leveraging appropriate activation authorities. Crisis response will be supported by 1st or 2d MEB.

- In the **NORTHCOM AOR,** units of I MEF, MARFORCOM/2d MEB, and MARFORRES may be tasked to provide support to civil authorities in response to national emergencies[8]. Additionally the Marine Corps supports theater security cooperation activities within NORTHCOM.

- **Crisis Response.** A crisis response force often must act with the forces on hand to protect national interests and preserve lives. Often this force must act before ideal conditions are met. Where A2/AD threats exist this requires projecting power from increased stand-off distances. A *force biased for action*, which is one of the eight attributes of Expeditionary Force 21, will be able to respond immediately. Non-combatant evacuation and disaster relief efforts—often complicated by the actions of state and non-state actors—will require rapid, timely responses from forward naval forces, sometimes into contested areas where adversaries seek to deny our ability to operate. As such, the Marine Corps will provide the Joint Staff with both forward-positioned crisis response forces and global response forces that are scalable, CONUS-based, and regionally oriented.

  This will include a CONUS-based crisis response task force—composed of a reinforced infantry battalion task force, aviation and logistics enablers—that can be fully deployed within 8-12 hours of notification. For larger crises, we will maintain a JTF-capable MEB CE that can deploy a 'suitcase staff' capable of taking command within 12 hours. By rapidly deploying a MEB CE, the Marine Corps will provide the means to effectively composite and command forward-deployed ARG/MEUs and SPMAGTFs, along with CONUS-based crisis response task forces, maritime prepositioning forces, and forces from other services or nations, as a cohesive organization.

Amphibious Warships in Support of Enhanced Posture. Amphibious warships are more than transports. As shown in Figure 9, they are versatile, interoperable warfighting platforms capable of going into harm's way and serving as a cornerstone of America's ability to project power and respond to a range of crises. With embarked Marines, amphibious ships are 'the Swiss Army knife of the fleet' providing diverse capabilities unlike any other naval platform. They are critical in providing seabased forces in theater to build partners and relations in key regions, deter aggression, defeat and deny

Amphibious Ship Capabilities

Foundation for seabasing
- Flight decks ...air mobility
- Well decks ... surface mobility
- Command and control suites
- Survivable in an anti-access environment
- Supporting forces for extended periods
- Flexible, rapid repositioning, self-sustaining

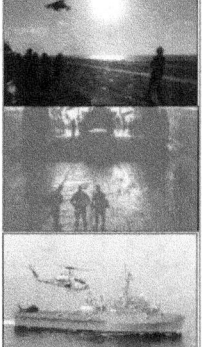

Figure 9: Expeditionary Operations ..."From the Sea"

sanctuary to terrorists, respond to crises and contingencies, and project power and influence globally. From forward presence to disaster response to power projection this is the one warship that very few

---

[8] Activation of reserve forces in response to national emergencies will generally be conducted via the involuntary mobilization authority vested in 10 U.S.C §12304a.

operations can be conducted without.

Historically, meeting each GCC demand for amphibious forces would require an inventory greater than 40 amphibious ships. Our naval requirement of 38 amphibious ships was developed on a capacity for forward presence, crisis response, and forcible entry operations. The naval forces have accepted risk with an inventory of 33 amphibious warships with 30 operationally available. We can meet the goals of Expeditionary Force 21 and provide a forward postured force responsive to GCC demand across the ROMO. This inventory level also provides the needed capacity for a MEB/Expeditionary Strike Group (ESG) to respond to a crisis or contingency within 25 days.

When the Nation requires a forcible entry capability, these same warships can embark, deploy, and employ the assault echelons of two MEBs, with some risk taken in the timely arrival of certain combat support elements. However, an inventory of fewer than 33 ships causes unacceptable risk in maintaining continuous presence and undermines the ability to generate the necessary capabilities to respond to crisis or conduct forcible entry. As our goal is to increase seabased forward deployed forces, we are examining how to mitigate that risk through the innovative integration and employment of alternative naval platforms and land basing.

3. Increasing Naval Integration

We will strengthen our partnership with the Navy, Coast Guard, and SOF by seeking ways to operate more effectively throughout the maritime domain, in both the seaward and landward portions of the littorals, and maximize the Marine Corps' footprint on available amphibious ships. We will address the operational integration of the MEB and the Navy Expeditionary Strike Group (ESG) and Carrier Strike Group (CSG). Additionally, Marine Corps and Navy components will coordinate with Coast Guard, Special Operations counterparts and regional partners to identify areas for increased integration in support of

Figure 10: Integrated Naval Force

GCC objectives, resulting in the more efficient application of limited naval resources. Furthermore, naval forces will continue to establish complementary relationships with SOF to give the GCCs increased capability and capacity options over the ROMO.

The maritime services are uniquely capable of using the sea and waterways as maneuver space, providing GCCs with persistent, self-sustaining, sea-based forces to meet the full spectrum of requirements. The tri-service *Maritime Security Cooperation Policy: An Integrated Navy-Marine Corps-Coast Guard Approach* enables coordination and integration across the three maritime services for the planning and conduct of theater-level security cooperation. In doing so, the GCCs gain more effective and efficient maritime force packages that increase the capability and capacity of partner nation maritime security forces and their supporting institutions, increase interoperability, and strengthen regional and global stability.

Closely intertwined with adjustments to forward posture is the ability to employ and sustain widely distributed units capable of performing tasks across the ROMO. There are many functional areas, CONOPS, and capabilities that will need to be examined to do this effectively. Some, like naval logistics integration, are already well advanced. Other capabilities need particular attention, with three standing at the forefront:

- Command and control.
- Marines operating from alternative platforms.
- Surface littoral maneuver capability.

Command and Control. To provide the unity of command necessary to operate most effectively in the maritime domain, afloat Marine Corps forces normally operate as part of larger naval task forces under a joint force maritime component commander (JFMCC) or fleet commander. To further enhance mutual understanding and unity of effort, we will increase the number of Marines assigned to the JFMCC and fleet staffs. Additionally, within functional and GCCs, Marine Corps component commanders will coordinate with their Navy and Coast Guard counterparts to integrate resources and supporting plans to produce more effective and efficient maritime force packages. We will also examine the level of organizational alignment at which integration should take place at subordinate echelons. As a starting point:

- For planning, training, and exercise purposes, each MEB CE will establish habitual relationships with the ESG, CSG, and other Navy counterparts aligned to the same region.
- For experimentation purposes, each MEB CE will explore staff integration during training and exercises with its equivalent Navy headquarters (e.g., NECC, ESG, CSG, JFMCC, etc.) to form 'littoral maneuver forces.'
- Creating integrated Blue/Green organizations will optimize the force for littoral operations and strengthen the ability of naval forces to respond to crises or conduct operations ashore. This innovation must be tempered by recognition that, for some missions, Marines may conduct sustained operations of increased duration ashore. As we seek to strengthen the Blue/Green team, we need to be mindful that we have to retain the ability to transition into an organization

Figure 11: Naval Force Poised for Action

  capable of conducting "such other duties as the President or Secretary of Defense may direct."
- The need for immediate action must be complemented by prudent steps to mitigate risk. Partnering with SOF and developing and employing Marine Corps reconnaissance will help the MEB to assess and/or shape the operating environment and seize critical infrastructure, key terrain, and lodgments for expeditionary bases. This includes seizing littoral terrain and denying its use by the enemy for sanctuary or use as a base for A2/AD systems.
- In coordination with Navy counterparts, we will explore the utility of establishing 'oceanic outposts' as an integral element of fleet efforts to counter A2/AD threats.

Alternative Ship Options. Amphibious ships provide the optimal means of employing Marines from the sea and are recognized as high-demand/low-density platforms. Given fiscal constraints, we need to recognize that there are not enough amphibious ships to meet all GCC operational demands. As a result, we need to modify traditional employment methods and augment amphibious warships by adapting other vessels for sea-based littoral operations. Reflective of Department of Defense guidance, PACOM and CENTCOM will continue to be the priority for the allocation of ARG/MEUs because they require the full range of capabilities inherent in these types of forces. Some operational requirements in those or other AORs may be satisfied by single amphibious ships or a combination of amphibious ships and alternative shipping adapted for Marine Corps capabilities.

The desired characteristics that may be resident or added to such platforms include: command and control capability; the ability to launch and recover aircraft; the ability to launch and recover surface vehicles or craft; medical capability; and billeting, messing, and sanitation capacity. Other considerations include: modification costs; additional manning requirements; impact on missions for which the vessel is primarily designed; operating range, endurance, and survivability.

Figure 12: Integrating Naval Platforms

Alternative platforms for potential exploration and experimentation include but are not limited to: surface combatants; the Mobile Landing Platform (MLP) enhanced as an afloat staging base; Littoral Combat Ships (LCS) with a habitability module; Joint High Speed Vessels (JHSV) with sufficient sea state and C4 capacity; high-speed transports; Maritime Prepositioning Squadron ships in combinations of T-AKE *Lewis and Clark*-class dry cargo ships or a Large Medium-speed Roll-on/Roll-off Ship (LMSR) with an MLP.

4. Enhancing Littoral Maneuver Capability

Amphibious operations[9] are often envisioned as amphibious assaults which, in turn, are widely misconstrued as involving large formations attacking frontally from the sea. While many World War II examples did indeed involve such attacks, this had more to do with the limitations imposed by geography and technology rather than poor tactics or a lack of imagination by the practitioners. In fact, pre-war Navy-Marine Corps doctrine clearly espoused using creative means to, "execute surprise landings at points where, due to the nature of the beaches or terrain, landings would not ordinarily be expected."[10] As Figure 13 below illustrates, the Naval team did just that in the July 1944 assault on Tinian, landing two divisions unopposed behind enemy defenses using two beaches that were only 60 and 160 yards wide—as opposed to the 1,300 to 2,500 yards used to land divisions in other operations in the face of the enemy.

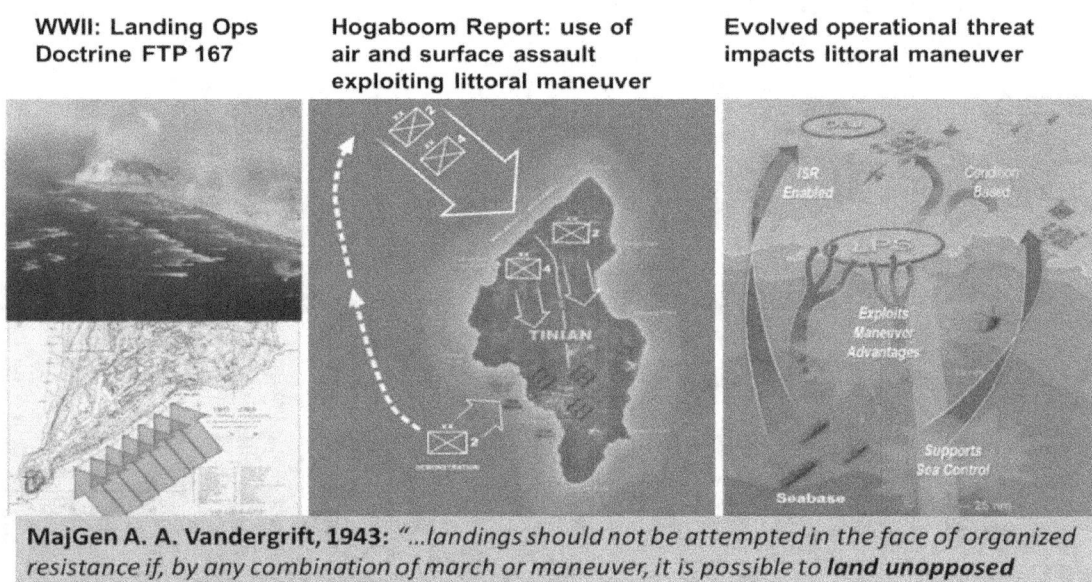

| WWII: Landing Ops Doctrine FTP 167 | Hogaboom Report: use of air and surface assault exploiting littoral maneuver | Evolved operational threat impacts littoral maneuver |

MajGen A. A. Vandergrift, 1943: "...landings should not be attempted in the face of organized resistance if, by any combination of march or maneuver, it is possible to **land unopposed within striking distance of the objective.**"

Figure 13: The Invasion of Tinian Exemplified Operational Maneuver in the Littorals

After World War II, the Marine Corps pursued the development of the helicopter as a tactical means to avoid fixed defenses, but the "Hogaboom Board" soon recognized that vertical maneuver capabilities alone would not fully replace surface maneuver, owing to weight and volume constraints. Since then, the Naval services have sought to develop complementary means of conducting vertical and surface littoral maneuver from increased distances, and via multiple penetration points, using the sea as maneuver space to offset the range and precision of modern weapons. In recent years, we have been very successful regarding vertical maneuver capabilities, but less so in the realm of surface maneuver. The Landing Craft Air Cushion (LCAC) has been effective but is nearing the end of its service life. Our recent attempts to field an affordable, high-speed, long-range amphibious vehicle capable of maneuver at sea and on land have not met the requirement. Fielding high-speed, long-range high-capacity system of connectors, amphibious vehicles, and boats are a critical necessity for amphibious operations.

---

[9] Per the Joint Publication 3-02, *Amphibious Operations*, (2009) there are five types of amphibious operations: 1. assault; 2. raid; 3. demonstration; 4. withdrawal; and 5. support to other operations. The forthcoming revision to that publication will revise the fifth type to "support to crisis response and other operations."

[10] See Fleet Training Publication 167, *Landing Expeditions Doctrine*, (1938), para 127/p. 9 and para 151/p.16, fig. 7.

Expeditionary Force 21

We will continue to conduct future amphibious operations at the time and place of our choosing. We will maneuver through the littorals to positions of advantage, employ disaggregated, distributed and dispersed forces to secure entry points that allow us to rapidly build our combat power ashore and allow for the quick introduction of follow-on joint/coalition forces to maintain momentum and expand the area of operation. Mindful of limitations on resources, we need to develop a viable combination of connectors, landing craft, amphibious vehicles, and boats, as well as the ships—to include the well decks or davits—that project them exploring a mix of surface maneuver options that:

- Are deployable, employable and sustainable given the power projection means available.
- Operate with reduced signature to multiple penetration points.
- In coordination with the Navy, employ low-signature landing craft and boats with increased range and speed, as well as the ability to penetrate an unimproved coastline.
- Provide the means to conduct surface maneuver from amphibious ships beyond 65 nm offshore.
- Provide the capability to maneuver through the complex terrain of the littorals.
- Provide a mechanism to identify, bypass, and if required breach shore-laid obstacle belts (explosive and non-explosive) to secure entry points.
- Provide maneuver options to extend operations within constraints of fuel resupply resources.
- Increase ability to work with space assets and develop capabilities within the cyber realm.

The increased likelihood of operations in the littorals requires a renewed focus on the Marine Corps' responsibility to be organized, trained and equipped, "for service with the fleet in the seizure and defense of advanced naval bases." The development and proliferation of A2/AD capabilities threaten freedom of action at sea and endanger the limited number of U.S. bases overseas. These conditions will require establishing advanced bases and austere expeditionary sites for employment of distributed STOVL operations as an enabler for sea control and power projection.

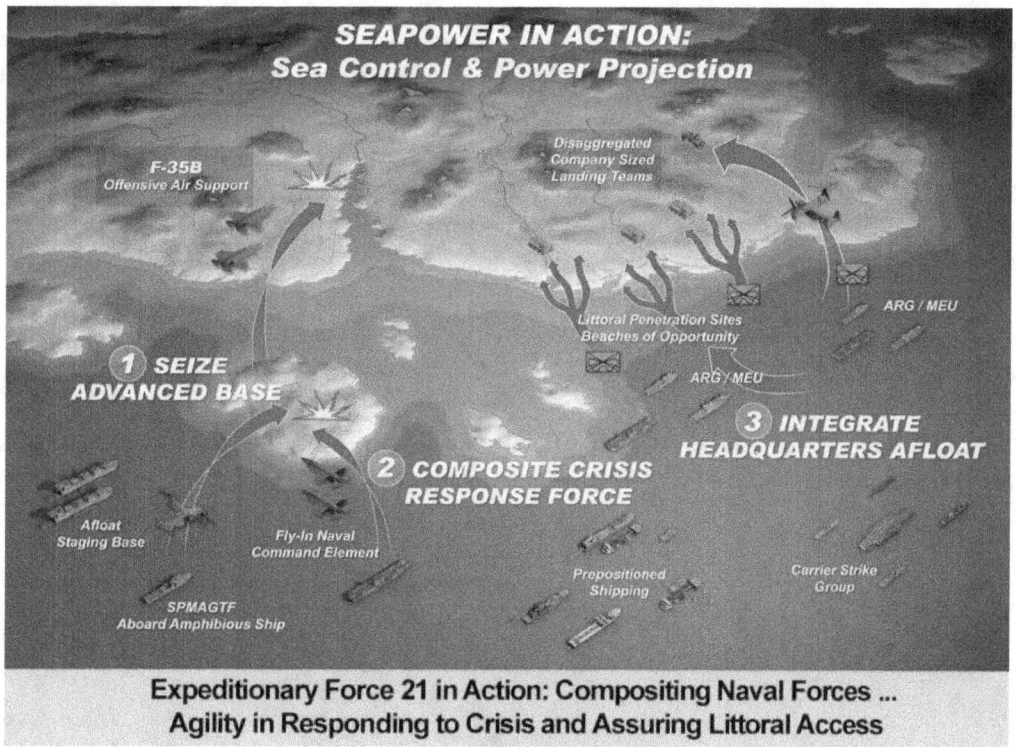

Figure 14: Integrated Naval Power

VII. Concept of Deployment and Employment

In an earlier era, the Marine Corps had a concise construct for deployment and employment: *"Deploy as MEBs, fight as a MEF."*

Under that construct, MEB-sized forces were task-organized and embarked aboard amphibious ships. They were complemented by Maritime Prepositioning Force (MPF) MEBs, or combined with multiple MPF MEBs to form MEFs. MEB-sized landing forces were task-organized and embarked in amphibious ships at their home stations and then deployed to a given AOR for operations. These amphibious forces were complemented by maritime prepositioning forces, which combined maritime prepositioning squadrons already postured in priority AORs with a fly-in echelon that conducted reception, staging, and onward movement via secure ports and airfields in the objective area. This construct worked exactly as envisioned during *Operation Desert Shield/Desert Storm*. Today's environment places increased emphasis on the GCCs' requirements for security cooperation and crisis response. Given these requirements, forward MEUs, SPMAGTFs, or other task-organized forces can be composited to form a MEB for immediate crisis and contingency response.

Expeditionary Force 21 evolves the Marine Corps construct for deployment and employment to: *"Deploy as SPMAGTFs and MEUs for steady-state engagement activities and crisis response, composite forward into a MEB for more significant crises and contingencies, expand the MEB into a MEF to fight major operations and campaigns."*

Formally stated, the MEB mission is to "provide a rapidly deployable and CJTF-capable command element with task-organized air-ground forces that are composited from forward-deployed and/or rapidly deployable forces in order to fulfill GCC requirements." The MEB is general officer-led and capable of providing an expeditionary force in readiness focused on security cooperation activities and exercises with partner nations, responding to crises, and projecting power while operating forward under the threat of potential adversaries. Thus, readiness for the MEB means being prepared for immediate, effective employment in any type of crisis or conflict. Underpinning this readiness is the ability to operate in contested environments and project power ashore in support of our national objectives. The relevancy of the MEB is directly related to its ability to rapidly respond and meet the GCCs' operational requirements from crisis response to forcible entry operations, with a special focus on crisis response. The MEB's ability to rapidly composite forces forward and project power to defeat adversaries enhances the strategic agility and operational reach of the naval enterprise.

On a day-to-day basis, the MEB CEs will maintain situational awareness within their designated AORs in close coordination with the respective regional MARFOR and Navy and SOF counterparts. When crises arise, the initial response force will likely consist of a forward ARG/MEU and/or SPMAGTF. For those crises that require a larger response, the MEB CE will rapidly deploy by air to a forward location either afloat or ashore to: assume command of Marine Corps forces already present and those soon to arrive, such as the MEU or CONUS-based crisis response task forces; provide a contributing portion of an integrated naval headquarters; or provide the nucleus of a JTF headquarters. In the event of major operations and campaigns, one or more MEBs may conduct missions such as forcible entry or, with the arrival of the higher headquarters, see the MEB CE expanded into a MEF CE.

Compositing the MEB. The concept for deploying the MEB has to accommodate the need to rapidly and effectively respond to a crisis. Figure 15 provides examples of compositing and employing the scalable MEB. The MEB will composite forward-deployed MAGTFs (such as MEUs and SPMAGTFs) and augment them with CONUS-based GRF as necessary. This composited MEB will most likely comprise some combination of forward-deployed forces, rapidly deploying forces, and land or maritime prepositioning forces. The specific combination of forces will depend upon, among other things, the mission, factors of time, distance, and strategic mobility resources available. In sum, the requirement to rapidly deploy a credible combat force in response to a crisis situation, within real-world lift constraints, will often drive the MEB to the formation and employment of composited forces.

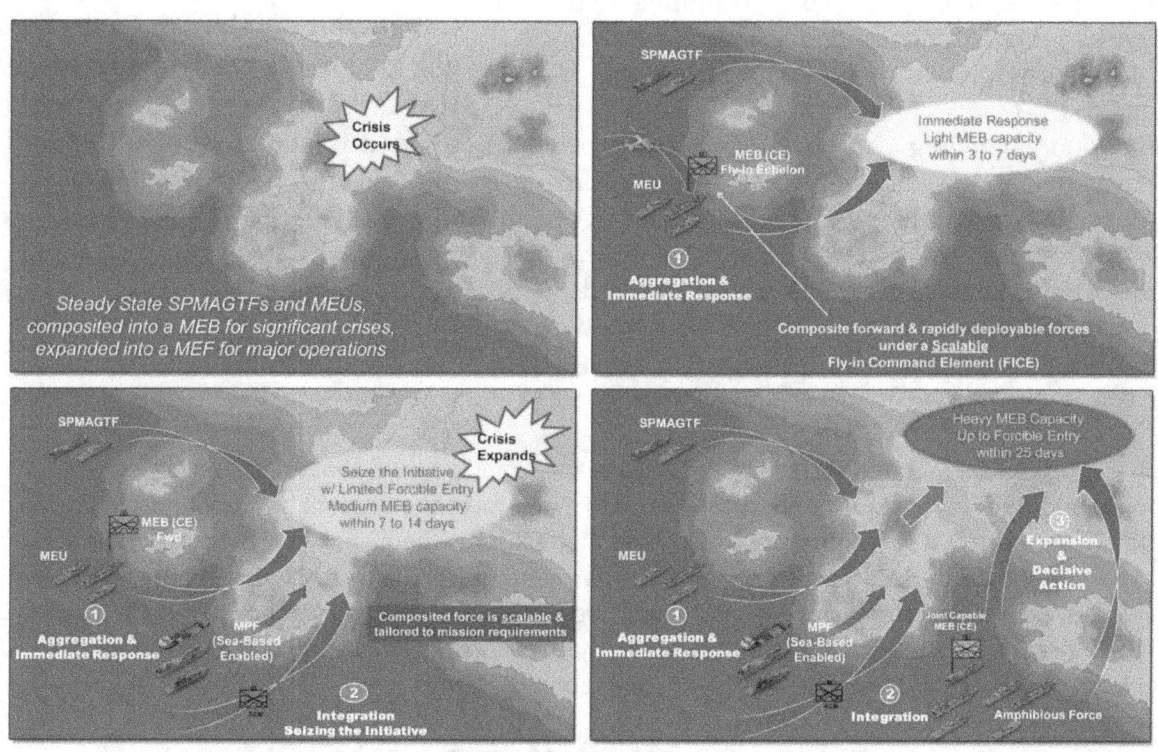

Figure 15: Compositing and Employing the Scalable MEB

Several constructs can be employed in forming the MEB. Our doctrinal model is based around a CE, regimental landing team, composite aviation group, and composite combat logistics regiment. However, given the environment and available lift when a crisis occurs beyond the scope of a forward MEU or SPMAGTF, forward forces will composite into a MEB focused on meeting the crisis. One method of initial compositing is to deploy the MEB CE and form the MEB with arriving units, leaving subordinate units intact with established command relationships. Another method is to designate a forward O-6 level MAGTF (i.e., MEU) as the base MAGTF for forming the MEB and form additional assets around that base unit. That base MAGTF is designated as the MEB (Fwd), and its commander is the MEB (Fwd) commander. A third method, employed in current OPLANs, is to composite the elements of the arriving forces into GCE, LCE, and ACE under the arriving MEB CE, in effect de-establishing the original units and creating a traditional MAGTF from the associated capabilities.

We have demonstrated the ability to composite forward forces in the past during the opening of *Operation Enduring Freedom* and entry operations by Task Force 58, as well as during relief operations in Haiti during 2010, where two ARG/MEUs composited. Further, we have recently shown the ability of a

JTF-capable CE to deploy rapidly and command composited forces during initial operations to resolve chaos and relieve suffering in *East Timor* in 1999, in response to the 2011 *earthquake and tsunami in Japan*, and most recently in the relief efforts in response to *Typhoon Haiyan in the Philippines*.

VIII. Summary

As stated in the Joint Operational Access Concept, as a global power with global interests the U. S. has an enduring requirement to project power and influence. The joint force will meet this requirement and its associated challenges through increased cross-domain synergy. The Marine Corps intends to contribute to this synergy as a forward and responsive naval force. The next 10 years promise to be a new and challenging venture as the Marines Corps reorganizes, refits, redefines our operational capabilities, and strengthens our naval roots. Some goals within Expeditionary Force 21 will be easily met; others we must strive hard to achieve. Given the fiscal austerity, we need to review capability development to minimize duplication and uncoordinated efforts. It is essential that we fully integrate naval capabilities and scrutinize everything from concept to doctrine to material requirement and solutions.

> **Geographic Combatant Commanders will gain the three-fold advantages of forward presence: the recurring dividends available from "soft power" applied with a richer military dimension; the deterrent effect of an immediate, credible and capable response; and the freedom of action**

Given this emphasis we intend to ensure a forward and ready posture that enables immediate crisis response and offers the ability to composite with forward forces to provide additional capability as needed to support GCC requirements. It is critical that we have the ability to prosecute combat operations throughout the littorals (land-sea-air) as an integrated naval force. By leveraging naval capabilities, developing the techniques for rapidly deploying and integrating forces and staffs, and developing required future capabilities, the Navy/Marine Corps team will be better positioned to provide the GCC with the forces in readiness to respond to crises.

Expeditionary Force 21 expands on certain concepts and provides the basis for future Navy/Marine Corps capability development to the meet the challenges of the 21st Century. The vision for Expeditionary Force 21 is to provide guidance for how the Marine Corps—as an integral part of the larger naval team—will be postured, organized, trained, and equipped to fulfill the responsibilities assigned to us, in public law and national policy, in the evolving security landscape. Through Expeditionary Force 21 we will:

- Focus on crisis response.
- Increase our emphasis on missions ranging from theater security cooperation through forcible entry.
- Enhance our ability to operate from the sea and take advantage of all platforms and means.
- Provide **the right force in the right place at the right time**.

> **"As America's Crisis Response Force We Are Organized, Trained and Equipped to Face Down the Threats of Our Time, Anywhere in the World, At a Moment's Notice."** —General James F. Amos,

Expeditionary Force 21

Implementation Plan for Developing Capabilities and Capacity

Today's and tomorrow's security environments require a reshaping of the Marine Corps with an emphasis on the growing demand for steady-state activities and crisis response. Our goals are designed to build the right force in the right place at the right time, today and in the next 10 years. This means we must develop solutions across the ROMO and for permissive, uncertain, and hostile environments. While some capabilities may require new equipment to achieve our goals; we must remain committed to working within fiscal and force structure limits. Each adjustment to capability must have an eye toward improving our ability to **deploy, employ, and sustain** as an expeditionary force. Our ability to achieve these goals and perform effectively will require increased integration as a naval and joint force. The key will be to develop our organic capabilities as an expeditionary force with an **increased capability to leverage other service and joint capabilities and capacities.**

> **Expeditionary Force 21** will produce a Marine Corps that ...
> - ✓ **Sustains an increased and enduring presence around the globe**
> - ✓ **Establishes Marine Expeditionary Brigades with a specific geographic orientation**
> - ✓ **Employs tailored regionally oriented forces that can rapidly respond to emergencies and escalating crises**
> - ✓ **Rapidly deploy tailored command and control packages – fully joint capable**
> - ✓ **Operates as part of a more integrated naval force to better fight and win complex conflicts throughout the littorals**

1. Overarching Guidance

In this time of fiscal austerity, we need to rethink how we form, train, equip, organize, and employ naval forces if we are to develop the capabilities and capacities envisioned under Expeditionary Force 21. We need to develop capabilities that enable new methods to meet demand and achieve operational goals. This starts with a shift in how we sustain a forward posture, meet the requirements of a crisis response force, composite forward to meet crises and contingencies and operate effectively in future contested environments. To realize the potential of Expeditionary Force 21, the Marine Corps must be innovative in its approach to capability development and relentless in mapping return on investment across the enterprise. Expeditionary Force 21 will assist in identifying and prioritizing capabilities and requirements (Task/Condition/Standard). These tasks, conditions, and standards for designated scenario(s) will be validated in recurring Marine Corps wargames.

Expeditionary Force 21 guidance will be reviewed and updated annually. This guidance is the common denominator between the Marine Corps Service Campaign Plan, Marine Corps Force Development System, and programmatic decisions as described below:
- Support the Marine Corps Strategic Health Assessment (MCSHA) and identify the delta between the capabilities of our current force and the capabilities required to achieve Expeditionary Force 21.
- Provide a means to synchronize advocate campaign plans.
- Provide a basis for capability development wargames.
- Evaluate approaches to assess effectiveness.
- Pursue an appropriate practical solution within the DOTMLPF-P spectrum.
- Validate the effort with senior leadership.

2. Assessment of Capability

In support of Expeditionary Force 21 development, an operational planning team (OPT) of senior subject matter experts (SMEs) representing Headquarters, U.S. Marine Corps (HQMC) departments and divisions, MARFORs, and other related organizations conducted a multi-day assessment to prioritize USMC Tier II capabilities and validate capability standards within the projected 10-year Expeditionary Force 21 future warfighting context and the above listed focus areas. The assessment focused on three scenarios spanning the range of likely military operations: 1) future steady-state activities described in Expeditionary Force 21; 2) a low-end crisis response structured around a humanitarian assistance and disaster relief scenario; and 3) a high-end response structured around a forcible entry scenario.

OPT members used the following documents and material in their prioritization assessments: "Attributes of Expeditionary Force 21" and USMC Tier II capabilities. "Attributes" descriptions were tailored for each scenario to assist OPT SMEs with identifying capability relevance in each scenario. The 46 Tier II capabilities included the 38 POM-16 approved Tier II capabilities (based on the Joint Capability Areas taxonomy) and eight capabilities (sea control; power projection; maritime security; integrated naval command and control; integrated naval logistics; enabling access; establishment of advanced bases; and using the sea as a base) added to address naval integration and expeditionary operations. OPT members worked from definitions and descriptions of each capability along with proposed standards based on the draft Expeditionary Force 21 document.

For each scenario, OPT members first assessed the relative importance/value of each of the eight "Attributes of Expeditionary Force 21" in conducting operations in that session's scenario. Then they assessed the importance/value of each of the 46 Tier II capabilities measured against each of the attributes and in the context of that particular scenario. At the end they also assessed the contribution/importance of each of the three scenarios for shaping and influencing future USMC capability development. A key result of this assessment is a prioritized list of the Tier II capabilities that the OPT believes should help guide USMC force design and development to maintain USMC relevance over the next 10 years in the context of a budget-informed and challenging future security environment. The following lists the top-10 prioritized Tier II capability (POM-16 Tier II Capability identification number or added capability) when viewed and weighted collectively through the lens of all three scenarios and all eight attributes:

1. Use the Sea as a Base
2. Power Projection
3. Maneuver Forces
4. Integrated Naval C2
5. Direct Execution
6. Force Preparation
7. Transport Information
8. Achieve Situational Awareness
9. Organize
10. Provide Deployment and Distribution Support

The complete priority list as well as tasks, conditions, and standards will be published online. This assessment and prioritization of higher level capabilities within the context of Expeditionary Force 21 provides necessary guidance between Marine Corps strategic planning and the force development and programming processes. They ensure the necessary linkage between immediate and future MAGTF warfighting requirements and balance them with supporting establishment requirements that sustain the Corps' institutional health. The capability assessment will be an annual process occurring within the August-September timeframe.

During this assessment risk was accepted in areas associated with sustained operations ashore whether for major combat or stability purposes (see Notional Joint Phasing Model; Phases III-V). The Expeditionary Force 21 goals and the capability assessment prioritized forward presence and crisis response up to the MEB level as further described within the focus areas below.

3. Focus Areas

a. Naval Integration. Achieving the vision of Expeditionary Force 21 will require greater integration of naval capabilities particularly in sea control, power projection, maritime security, and integrated maritime command and control. Integration is defined as "the arrangement of military forces and their actions to create a force that operates by engaging as a whole." Integration can be achieved by combining multiple separate forces or organizations into one, or by better aligning separate forces or organizations with one another. The first method will provide both unity of effort and command, the second will enable greater unity of effort. Both methods will improve the effectiveness and efficiency of naval forces operating within the projected future operating environment.

Naval forces normally employ sea control and power projection as an indivisible whole. For example, gaining sea control may be dependent upon power projection in the form of strikes and amphibious raids to neutralize land-based threats to the fleet, or amphibious assaults to seize and control littoral terrain such as islands, archipelagos, straits, or shorelines. Naval power projection capabilities underpin a broad spectrum of missions by allowing us to rapidly insert, support, and when appropriate, withdraw forces ashore; provide sea-based intelligence, surveillance and reconnaissance (ISR) and fire support to forces ashore; conduct riverine operations; and establish lodgments to facilitate the introduction of additional forces.

At the heart of naval integration lie command arrangements that foster cooperative naval solutions at the institutional, operational, and tactical level:

- At the institutional level, greater alignment between the HQMC and OPNAV staff directorates, along war-fighting functions, will promote greater understanding and stronger relationships between the multiple principal staffs directly responsible to service leadership.
- At the operational level, Marine, Navy, and Coast Guard components will integrate resources in a manner that provides the GCC with the most responsive and effective support from the maritime domain.
- Integrating plans between the regional MARFORs, Navy, and Coast Guard components will better posture the maritime services to develop robust, multi-year plans that ensure the most efficient use of limited security cooperation resources. This will involve naval integration with the Theater Special Operations Command (TSOC) and developing a foundation for integration into the JFMCC staff and Maritime Operations Centers.
- At the tactical level, MEF, MEB, Fleet, and ESG headquarters, should develop the same degree of the robust integration and interoperability of the ARG/MEU.

- Navy, Marine Corps, and Coast Guard expeditionary forces can further integrate functions such as beach master and landing support, and small boats and riverine units, much like medical and tactical air integration today.

More closely integrating naval capabilities across the institutional, operational, and tactical level should focus on enhancing the following areas:

- Expeditionary ISR, organic fixed-wing strike, long-range assault support, and cyber/electronic warfare (EW) operations, all of which are critical to conducting strikes and amphibious raids to neutralize land-based threats to the fleet.
- Training and education, exercises and deployments that expand Blue/Green staff relationships to foster greater unity of effort, increased speed of action, and seamless execution of sea control.
- The ability to conduct amphibious assaults to seize, secure and or control littoral terrain such as islands, archipelagos, straits, or shorelines and deny its use to an adversary.
- The ability to plan and manage fuel resupply requirements at the operational and theater level, enabled by sustainment command and control relationships.
- The ability to maneuver throughout the entire littoral battlespace (air, land, sea), including along restrictive waterways; to conduct expeditionary strikes and raids; establish multiple expeditionary airfields and bases; and provide the unity of command necessary to operate effectively in the maritime domain.
- Maritime security which involves: increased planning, coordination and exercises to integrate Marine capabilities into the Navy's composite warfare concept (CWC); boarding capabilities from multiple platforms and forces; improved employment of USMC rotary-wing assets in support of the naval maritime security mission; and improved training, planning, and coordination with the U.S. Coast Guard operational commanders.
- A coordinated approach to ensuring readiness of platforms and forces to achieve GCC goals.

b. Conducting Security Cooperation. The Marine Corps conducts security cooperation activities to build the capacity of partner nations' security forces; build/establish relationships; and facilitate or provide access. The activities envisioned as a key contribution of Expeditionary Force 21 to meet GCC requirements involve actions associated with security cooperation with partner nations. Security cooperation provides a means for forward-deployed forces to prevent or mitigate conflict at a reasonable cost. Building partner capacity often results in more responsible, competent security forces, able to resolve a local crisis before it becomes a threat to U.S. interests and requires intervention. Security cooperation also positions U.S. forces for potential military operations by fostering interoperability with future coalition partners, increasing operational access, and providing opportunities for sustainment training.

The Marine Corps tailors its general purpose forces to meet evolving GCC requirements. Marine Corps forces receive training appropriate to the AOR to which they deploy, and are supported with the required enabling capabilities. Force options include: training teams, task forces, and MAGTFs. MAGTFs most frequently utilized for security cooperation are SPMAGTFs and MEUs. SPMAGTFs for both crisis response and theater security cooperation are constructed to meet the needs of a particular region, are sea and/or land based, and support GCC objectives by conducting a range of activities such as the training of foreign security forces, multinational exercises, and information sharing. MEUs focus on crisis response. The MEU's primary steady-state activities are deterrence and forward presence, but MEUs also conduct a range of security cooperation activities with a focus on multinational exercises and other activities that enhance interoperability with capable partner nation forces.

Expeditionary Force 21 expands on recent experience as well as on-going regional activities. Capability development to promote partnership building should focus on:

- Imparting proven methods to support staffs and forces in Expeditionary Force 21's regionally oriented MEBs, SPMAGTFs, and MEUs.
- Enhancing integration with regional components.
- Maintaining institutional security cooperation/security force assistance knowledge and capability by continuing to emphasize task-organized forces enabled by dedicated security cooperation activities.
- Institutionalizing and increasing engagement and Information Operations (IO) training requirements for a larger number of deployable units to include employment of alternative shipping and alternative force compositions.
- Supporting MEUs and SPMAGTFs with deployable teams from the Marine Corps Information Operations Center (MCIOC).
- Ensuring Navy, Coast Guard, and Marine Corps forward-deployed forces gain and maintain regional understanding and awareness through liaison with the regional MARFOR and greater integration with TSOCs and their persistently deployed teams within priority nations in each AOR.

c. Maneuver. Operating in the littoral environment demands a Marine Corps with maneuver options in permissive, uncertain and hostile environments. These capabilities must be optimized to be deployed, employed and sustained with available lift and power projection means. Regardless of the level of threat amphibious forces must have the capability to penetrate a coastline and move inland through complex terrain.

In a contested environment—with increasingly capable adversaries equipped with coastal defense cruise missiles (CDCM) and other area denial capabilities—naval forces employ sea control and power projection in a complementary manner. Projecting and sustaining power ashore requires access to or control of the adjoining seas. However, sea control operations may require the projection of power ashore to remove threats to naval forces, or to control littoral terrain such as islands, archipelagos, straits, or shorelines.

In today's world, the likelihood of concurrent and geographically dispersed crises places a premium on forward-deployed forces that are versatile and mobile enough to respond to a range of missions in varied locations, and then reinforce and sustain operations. By providing a scalable first-response capability to protect U.S. citizens and interests, forward deployed forces provide time for national decision makers to evaluate follow on options. As such, responding to crises may require maneuver from increased distance under less than certain conditions. In these situations mission success may be time critical.

Considerations for Maneuver to Gain Entry Where Access is Denied. Forward-deployed crisis response forces most often operate within the threat of A2/AD systems daily and must be equipped, trained, and practiced to accomplish power projection under varied degrees of that threat. While we operate today in this environment, our goal is to increase our capability. The following considerations represent situations that we will prepare for and are a departure from previous norms:

- Crisis response involves a 'come as you are' dimension that may not allow for initial defeat of all A2/AD systems. As such, local air and maritime superiority may not be achieved prior to power projection.
- Crisis response and/or gaining local air and maritime superiority may require power projection to identify and reduce threats, which requires the ability to project power from greater ranges.
- Stand-off range for amphibious operations requires a careful calculus that includes battlespace geometry, risk, threat, and conditions with the following implications:
  - An integrated A2/AD threat with CDCMs necessitates standoff range greater than previously considered.
  - The proliferation of CDCMs and sophisticated target acquisition and guidance systems requires standoff from beyond 65nm until the threat is mitigated.
  - Once the CDCM threat is reduced, standoff can also be reduced. If a CDCM threat remains standoff can be reduced to a sea echelon area 30nm to 50nm to provide standoff from area denial threats, adequate CDCM acquisition, and protection by DDG/CGs. As mentioned above this is always a careful calculation of risk by the involved commanders.
  - Once landing sites are controlled, amphibious ships may close to facilitate speed of build-up ashore. When a CDCM threat is completely neutralized, an amphibious ship can reduce the standoff distance when provided appropriate escorts to mitigate any residual risk. The discharge point for Amphibious Assault Vehicles (AAVs) and other surface connectors may be closer to shore, but generally will remain beyond 12nm. When the threat as a whole is sufficiently mitigated as agreed upon by the commanders concerned, these ships may decrease standoff to support continued operations.
  - Landing site superiority must be established during amphibious operations requiring control of seaward approaches, landing areas, and the ability to inhibit threat actions.
  - Vehicles, boats, and landing craft require the endurance and speed to operate from 65nm independently or in combination with other connectors.
- Operating in dispersed formations, including the use of company-sized landing teams, is a means to counter increased enemy ISR and strike capabilities.
- The ability to identify, classify, bypass, and when necessary breach obstacles within the littoral.
- The ability to overcome ground obstacles (explosive and non-explosive) from the seaward approach when they cannot be by-passed during an assault.

The Amphibious Capabilities Working Group (ACWG) report pointed to the need for assessing surface connectors in light of the increased standoff and weight of MAGTF equipment. Additionally, the requirement for increased presence demands an examination of connectors, for range, capacity and ability to interface with all amphibious ships and MPS platforms. The ability to operate independently for extended periods would assist in distributed operations. With these increased standoff requirements, we need to develop new surface connectors with: greater capacity, increased range, and speed (18 knots, minimum, to ensure timely maneuver); reduced signature; and modular capabilities. New surface connectors must support at-sea transfer from the MLP and other platforms in order to support distributed operations, fires, logistics, and intelligence. To provide range and speed requirements, we need to explore boats for use in securing landing sites and littoral patrolling. These same boats can provide options for maneuver inland particularly in the Pacific, West Africa, and South America.

Considerations for Maneuver Inland. Once ashore, Marines require the ability to transit complex littoral terrain. Mobility options from the sea echelon areas must support maneuver inland via surface and air to inland entry points. This will require a combination of capabilities including but not limited to:

- A minimum capability to maneuver two battalion landing teams in armored personnel carriers per brigade amphibious assault echelon and up to 12 battalions in operations ashore.
- Maneuver from distributed entry points to concentrate forces and disperse as required.
- Ground combat and tactical vehicles that value land and water mobility performance and drive a subordinate but effective balance of lethality and protection.
- Surface connectors to bring Marines, weapons, vehicles, and large-footprint materiel ashore.
- Ground combat and tactical vehicle requirements that value transportability and sustainability.
- Ensuring in-stride obstacle breaching capabilities are maintained with future ground vehicle development.
- New ground maneuver platforms that can be transported internally via MV-22 or CH-53.
- New vessels to enable greater maneuver throughout the littoral and along inland waterways.

d. Fires. Fire support improvements involve platforms, munitions and systems for fire support coordination and responsiveness. The F-35B provides both a significant level of situational awareness as well as being a platform for responsive, scalable firepower. Rotary-wing close air support (CAS) assets and Joint Terminal Attack Controllers (JTACs) and indirect fires add further capability for precise, lethal fires. Enhancements are required to provide responsive, all-weather fire support options to forces maneuvering from the sea and in support of dispersed formations. These capabilities must be scalable in range, portable and lethal, with the ability to incorporate non-lethal operations such as Information Operations, Cyberspace Operations, and Electronic Warfare. Specific considerations for Expeditionary Force 21 include:

- The capability to employ HIMARS from distributed locations and naval platforms or surface connectors to support distributed maneuver.
- The continued development of long-range precision fire capabilities for the Expeditionary Fire Support System, the M777, and HIMARS from austere and expeditionary bases.
- The range and capacity to provide fires supporting multiple entry points from the sea.
- Enhanced munitions to increase naval surface fires capability and range.
- Increased capability of sensors to provide a target location of useable accuracy.
- Increased capacity to employ unmanned aerial system (UAS) from naval platforms and connectors supporting timely target acquisition.
- Increased capability from UAS to acquire targets, control fires, and deliver munitions.
- Enhanced ability to leverage joint fires in a timely manner from a distributed or concentrated force.
- Enhancement of naval surface fires to protect and support maneuver from 65 nm out to sea to inland objectives (including exploration of rail gun and laser technology).
- Enhanced integration of all systems to neutralize G-RAMM threats.

e. Command and Control / NET Centric. Given the anticipated complexity, tempo, and distributed nature of future power projection operations, naval forces will require both advanced information technology and flexible command relationships to support an increased level of coordination and integration among all elements of the force. We will need improved integration with garrison-like non-classified internet protocol network (NIPRNET) and secret internet protocol network (SIPRNET) network management tools, processes, images, configurations, and computers. Naval forces will require the ability to collect, process, and disseminate relevant information in near real-time to support distributed fire and maneuver at the operational and tactical levels.

This will require ISR sensors, processing systems and associated collaboration and communication systems to be fully interoperable and scalable to the particular mission. Platforms will be networked to allow for dispersed operations. Planning will be distributed using en-route mission planning software and leveraging reach-back to non-deployable organizations for subject matter expertise and expanded capacity. Given the distances from which they will be employed, naval forces will require collaborative planning, rehearsal, execution and assessment tools. Additionally, landing forces and support craft will require beyond-line-of-sight, over-the-horizon, and networked on-the-move systems capable of operating in a degraded communications environment.

To support Expeditionary Force 21, development of improved command and control capabilities both afloat and ashore must consider:

Organizational Change:

- Reduction from three to two deployable MEF HQs.
- MEF and MEB HQs that are JTF-capable with required joint augmentation and training. MEB command elements regionally oriented on planning and exercising command and control of forces conducting theater security cooperation and crisis response operations.
- MEBs that provide a rapidly deployable and Combined Joint Task Force (CJTF)-capable CE to include, depending on the crisis, a small 'suitcase staff' deployable within 12 hours.
- Ability to deploy augments to build up a MEB within a response time of 7 days and up to 25 days (depending on mission).
- Establishment of forward-postured SPMAGTFs to support security cooperation activities with partner nations and immediate response to episodic crises.
- Development of doctrine and training to composite MAGTFs.
- Enabling Navy and Marine Corps forward-deployed forces to gain and maintain regional understanding and awareness through liaison with the regional MARFOR and greater integration with TSOCs.

Impact of Organizational Changes:

- Doctrine and training to extend the scalability of the MEB and enhance fluid compositing of forces.
- Methods and processes to gain and employ regional understanding and awareness in an operationalized manner.

Changes to C2 Execution:

- Ability to control air and surface landing sites and dispersing and concentrating as needed to achieve military objectives at sea and on land across the modern littoral environment.
- Initiatives such as a naval fly-in command element and Cyber Electromagnetic Warfare Coordination Cell require exploration and development.
- Improve communications robustness within and to/from the MAGTF to ensure the reliable flow of information in a cyber-contested environment. Includes:
  - Terrestrial communications system with a 65 nm minimum range via line of sight, retransmission, relay, or combinations of all three means.

- Ability to send limited data via a terrestrial communications system or systems with a 65 nm minimum range via line of sight, retransmission, relay, or combinations of all three means.
- Reduce systems with redundant and/or overlapping capabilities in order to streamline maintenance, training, and increase efficiency and effectiveness across the MAGTF.
- Explore the use of ground communication systems aboard Navy shipping, specifically in the landing force operations center and the supporting arms control center.
- Ability to provide adaptive, distributed, cooperative, and collaborative decision-making and planning.
- Improving system interoperability and security across all domains and between forces from other Services.
- Improving access to timely and understandable information across all domains, with other services, and allied/coalition forces.

Net-Centric Focused Changes:

- Providing landing forces and support craft with beyond-line-of-sight, over-the-horizon, and on-the-move C2 systems capable of operating in a satellite-degraded communications environment.
- Providing a capabilities-based portfolio of tactical networking equipment and resources that, through the utilization of interoperable 'building blocks', provides the flexibility and scalability necessary to enable dispersed operations and support the compositing of MEB-level C2 forward.
- All networks will employ state-of- the-art cyberspace capabilities.
- Improving the ability to share situational awareness and mitigate current, significant gaps in up-to-date intelligence products sourced from commercial, coalition, interagency, and DOD systems and processes.
- Extending and protecting critical expeditionary enterprise services across the broader global system of bases, sites, and forward-deployed MAGTFs.
- Ensuring these services are interoperable with the joint enterprise.

f. Cyberspace and the Electromagnetic Spectrum. Freedom of action in cyberspace and the electromagnetic spectrum (EMS) is a key enabler to 21st century military operations. MAGTF operations depend upon cyberspace and the EMS.

Adversaries will seek to gain cyberspace superiority by exploiting the porous nature of the domain and making use of disruptive, game-changing technologies to stage operations in cyberspace at the time and place of their choosing. MAGTF commanders must confront and contest these adversaries in cyberspace to counter any potential operational advantage they might have. There are three critical challenges that must be considered when developing these capabilities:

- Understand that activities and operations in cyberspace not only support objectives within the domain itself, but also the other domains.
- The MAGTF must plan for and manage operational dependencies, vulnerabilities, and opportunities available in cyberspace and the EMS to execute C2, maneuver, fires, and gain awareness.
- Integrating and synchronizing cyberspace and EMS operations will be critical to mission success.

Doctrine for Cyberspace Operations and EMS Operations has undergone initial development and the Marine Corps are implementing a key component with the development of the Cyber Electronic Warfare Coordination Cell (CEWCC). The CEWCC coordinates the integrated planning, execution, and assessment of cyberspace and EMS operations across the MAGTF's operational environment to increase operational tempo and achieve military advantage. The MAGTF commander uses the CEWCC to ensure all organic and non-organic cyberspace and EMS-dependent capabilities are planned, executed, and assessed during all phases of an operation; and are incorporated into the MAGTF's operational design, concept of operations (CONOPS), scheme of maneuver, concept of fires support, intelligence operations, as well as in appropriate detailed plans and annexes. Additionally, the CEWCC provides an enhanced MAGTF capability for planning, requesting, and coordinating non-organic 'reach-back' support from external agencies to include Special Technical Operations. Because this support often requires long lead times and extensive coordination with national-level agencies, MAGTFs will rely heavily upon the CEWCC during deliberate planning, inter-deployment periods, and during preparation for deployment.

g. Force Protection. Force Protection (FP) needs increase as the force is positioned forward and disperses for littoral operations. The Marine Corps relies on mobility to execute its missions, and as forces maneuver, FP challenges generally increase and warrant improved planning and more effective capabilities. Multiple perimeters and extended lines of communication require a robust and detailed FP plan. Of particular concern is protection against area denial threats to amphibious ships and connectors transiting the littorals to landing sites. **Control of the landing site is essential regardless of means of entry and a critical condition for maneuver inland.** FP is not the mission; rather it is an integrated aspect of MAGTF operations. FP is achieved by the commander through the combined integration of the elements of combat power (protection, movement, maneuver, intelligence, fires, sustainment, and C2). Technology and unit/individual vigilance protect against enemy attack. Aggressive action produces a form of protection. Recent operations have shown that Marine units should refrain from 'hunkering down' and pro-actively interface with local populations to build relationships that provide force protection through information sharing.

Under the Expeditionary Force 21 concept, the MEB as part of an integrated naval force is capable of maneuvering with reduced signature from greater distance and conducting dispersed operations. The associated FP considerations include:

- Conducting integrated naval operations to protect the 'Seabase' from all threats.
- Projecting protection from the sea to extend over naval forces maneuvering inland.
- Defending the MAGTF from ground, air (includes counter UAS), missile, and cyber-attack.
- Increasing the ability to conduct populace control through capabilities such as identity operations and non-lethal means.
- Detecting and neutralizing CBRNE.
- Detecting and neutralizing explosive hazards, including mines, improvised explosive devices, unexploded ordnance, and explosive remnants of war.
- Employing passive and active systems for counter-adversary ISR deception, signature management, and decoys.
- Increased naval integration of USMC F-35B and USMC R/W assets while deployed forward on amphibious ships to counter A2/AD threats.

h. Intelligence. Intelligence is an indispensable Marine Corps Warfighting Function. Our modern expeditionary warfighting concepts increasingly depend on operating with precision, within an increasingly complex environment in which robust ISR operations are essential to mission success.

Scalable, ready forces require intelligence sensors, equipment, architectures, and tradecraft to establish and maintain battlespace awareness, influence the operating environment, and support decision-making at the point of attack. The Marine Corps Intelligence, Surveillance, and Reconnaissance Enterprise (MCISRE) develops, delivers, operates, and sustains fully integrated ISR capabilities to meet that requirement. Operating across all warfighting functions, the MCISRE provides commanders and decision-makers the intelligence information required to successfully plan and execute MAGTF missions. MCISRE effectiveness is enhanced through cooperation with interagency, joint, allied, and coalition partners. The ability to support real-time decision-making is predicated on a variety of massed and layered sensors, UAS, a robust architecture, and advanced analytical capabilities, combined with seamless national and theater intelligence structures, from CONUS to deployed tactical units. The MCISRE supports Marine Operating Force commanders in accordance with several key concepts.

Operations and Intelligence Integration. Recent operational experience has demonstrated a transformation in the relationship between operations and intelligence. Decisive knowledge at the point of action demands full integration of intelligence with operations across all echelons of command. When operations and intelligence are not integrated, intelligence does not receive the direction needed to be effective, and operations do not receive intelligence required for mission success. Institutional approaches must be fine-tuned to organize and train personnel in operations and intelligence integration to enable full fluency in this symbiotic relationship for all MAGTF mission sets.

Projecting ISR into Forward Operating Environments. MAGTF operations today, and in the future, will remain heavily dependent on garrison structure and access to the National Intelligence Community to project ISR capabilities to the tactical edge. Projecting the ISR warfighting function is much more than 'reach-back'. It is a scalable and planned progression of capabilities into the operational environment. Marine Corps Intelligence Centers (MICs) located at MEF Headquarters are networked to the Marine Corps Intelligence Activity (MCIA) and subordinate intelligence entities. As a fundamentally new way of doing business, continuously operating MICs become the surge, bounding, and recovery capability for current operations, as well as a global Indications and Warning node, where the MICs bridge multiple (national, theater, service) intelligence architectures to compensate for limited afloat bandwidth, billets, and shipboard spaces. As forces move ashore, MIC capability surges forward, consistent with the tactical footprint. With access to the MICs, deployed forces are able to focus on the current intelligence picture and tactical analysis. MCISRE capacity will provide commanders the best available intelligence while leveraging the entire intelligence community and theater assets.

Persistent ISR, Sensors, and Battlespace Awareness. Under Persistent ISR, the MAGTF commander is supported by intelligence collection assets organic to the MAGTF, with direct support from joint, and national resources, and Combat Support Agencies. Persistence is achieved through integrated, synchronized management and employment of the ISR Enterprise, to include all intelligence disciplines, ground reconnaissance, combat patrols, human intelligence (HUMINT), signals intelligence (SIGINT), UAS, aviation, space, and cyber. Capturing information in real-time is fundamental to persistent ISR. This necessitates data interoperability and direct communications between systems and collectors to enable integration of information, sensor cross-cueing, and fusion of multi-discipline/multi-source data as well as spatial and temporal visualization. Traditional and nontraditional battlefield sensors and activities should be linked by a sensing strategy that combines all sensor data, creating a Persistent ISR presence that transforms into battlespace awareness.

Intelligence Dissemination and Utilization (IDU). IDU is the identification and conveyance of relevant combat information and intelligence to satisfy a valid MAGTF intelligence requirement. IDU requires continuous feedback to ensure the right combat information and intelligence flows to the right consumer at the right time for actions or decisions. IDU must provide for access and dissemination of intelligence from multiple sources, including those external to the MAGTF. These resources may include, but are not limited to, Joint, Coalition, and national capabilities. IDU supports both the sharing and the protection of information, to include a capability to address multilevel security requirements.

Advanced Intelligence Analysis. Decision advantage in combat is a function of rapidly acquiring high-value information, performing quick and accurate analysis, and achieving immediate dissemination in the language of operations to generate speed in decision, higher-tempo operations, and combat effectiveness. Increasing the acquisition, analysis, processing, and dissemination in support of the commander's needs is how the Marine Corps will outmaneuver expected future threats despite the diffusion of advanced weapons, global surveillance, and networking. To achieve the higher levels of speed and precision, the MCISRE and its Navy and Coast Guard counterparts must provide a trained workforce that is skilled in the procedures of creating combat intelligence.

Supporting the full range of MAGTF missions, the MCISRE provides commanders and decision-makers the intelligence required for successful planning and execution. Under Expeditionary Force 21 these key capabilities must be enhanced:

- Operations and Intelligence Integration.
- Projecting ISR into forward operating environments.
- Persistent ISR, Sensors, and Battlefield Awareness.
- Intelligence Dissemination and Utilization.
- Advanced Intelligence Analysis.
- Fusion and dissemination of timely intelligence to smaller and distributed units.
- The use of intelligence liaisons or a fusion group in operations centers to speed the process of information dissemination and response to commander's priorities and information requirements.

i. Expeditionary Logistics. Our logistics capabilities supporting amphibious and prepositioning operations have successfully met the demands of today's security environment and now they must be more integrated to support steady-state operational requirements that will only increase in the future.

To meet future sustainment needs for distributed operations, the Marine Corps is expanding the capability to provide initial expeditionary logistics from a seabase outside the range of potential adversarial A2/AD capabilities. Our forward-deployed amphibious ships and positioned MPSRONs provide our MAGTFs with self-sustained capabilities for both aviation and ground with their initial expeditionary focused logistic capacities. They play key roles in our CONOPS for Expeditionary Sustainment in the Littorals that must cover both deployment and employment support.

Seabased Logistics is the operational and tactical sustainment process for naval maneuver warfare. As such, it can significantly enable actions for a JTF Commander based on primacy of the seabase, reduction in logistics demand, and the execution of continuous sustainment, resulting adaptive response and joint operations capabilities, as well as the ability to close and reconstitute forces at sea. Seabased Logistics employs logistic tactics, techniques, and procedures that deliver flexible, highly responsive support to better enable naval and joint operations. Resulting logistics will be effects-based so that supported operations, of whatever size, can result in specific desirable enabling reactions vice a massive logistic force centered on pre-planned resupply

Expeditionary Force 21

As an expeditionary force, whether in permissive, uncertain or hostile environments, our logistics concept of support and resulting capabilities will always take into account the levels of sustainment (e.g., Days of Supply / Days of Ammunition -- DOS/DOA) embarked as Accompanying Supplies and their control during the deployment, employment, and redeployment of Marine forces. Such levels of sustainment provide a ready, integrated, and capable force to a Geographic Combatant Commander...upon their arrival. In each phase, we will ensure that our naval logistics capabilities improve on our operational flexibility and scalability. Mission factors, operational lift allocation/apportionment, and/or supply availability may also make it necessary to adjust the balance between accompanying supplies and resupply, which has specific and deliberate impacts on a MAGTF's deployment and availability to sustain once employed.

- **SPMAGTF** – Whether task-organized for crisis response or theater security cooperation missions, these forces will deploy with limited organic maintenance and not less than 3 DOS/DOA of sustainment in terms of accompanying supplies. The most likely COA for SPMAGTF sustainment support is a combination of leveraged tactical organic/host nation (HN) support/contracted logistics and sustainment support coordinated for by the respective combatant commander MARFOR.

- **MEU** - This global response and forward presence MAGTF typically deploys with an organic maintenance and sustainment capability and Accompanying Supplies that provide up to 15 DOS/DOA that can be loaded on assigned shipping. With the increase in disaggregated and split operations, embark spaces to include that for sustainment, will need to be adjusted as mission(s) change and forces with their equipment cross-deck. The capacities of the Combat Logistics Force (CLF), in coordination with the Fleet, will maintain the sustainment capabilities needed across the MAGTF elements, attached Navy units, and supported SOF units as directed.

- **MEB** – Whether Amphibious or Maritime Prepositioned, MEBs will have accompanying supplies that provide up to 30 DOS/DOA for their initial sustainment. If a MEB is formed from the compositing of MEUs, their aggregated accompanying supplies and naval logistics gives the MEB its operating endurance until a viable theater logistics capability is available. Marine staff planners should re-acquaint themselves with the logistics support implications of the Assault Follow-on Echelon (AFOE) grounded by joint doctrine, policies, and procedures. Of note, sustainment stocks aboard amphibious ships are never zeroed out -- naval logistics does not wait until stocks are exhausted to replenish. They are constantly restocked or resupplied through underway replenishment (e.g., CONREP -- connected replenishment and/or VERTREP – vertical replenishment using helicopters). This unique capability ensures that naval forces are ready and available for mission or employment changes.

- **MEF** – A MEF does not deploy at once but employs as a result of compositing forward-deployed MAGTFs and those MAGTFs formed and deployed upon crisis execution. It is the aggregation of these MAGTFs' Accompanying Supplies and resupply by naval logistics that gives a MEF its initial endurance until Theater Logistics is available and functioning by joint and/or allied forces. The MEF can then remain in-theater to conduct the full range of military operations in support of the joint campaign.

Naval Logistics Integration (NLI) already provides significant benefits to afloat MEUs measured in terms of both cost efficiency and operational effectiveness. NLI is essential to the integration of processes and capabilities of both services plus the Coast Guard to source Marine Corps demand items from Navy stocks to include use of the combat logistics force ships to resupply both services.

A major corollary to seabasing is the reduction of the logistics footprint ashore. The former footprint must be reduced and will move to the seabase. The new footprint will be characterized largely as a transportation/distribution system that delivers seabased supplies to smaller and significantly dispersed units. Logistics 'pull' from ashore, as opposed to the 'push' characterized by the land-based stockpile approach, will be facilitated by naval total asset visibility linked to the operational (theater) and strategic levels, the capability to selectively offload at sea, and the ability to respond to/support a fast and changing tempo of operations.

By keeping much (though not necessarily all) of the supplies and support activities at sea in littoral operations, naval expeditionary forces will both reduce the vulnerability of logistics operations to enemy attack and allow greater maneuverability of forces ashore. A small combat service support area ashore may be needed or several similar sized areas based on the force distribution, threat, and/or operating areas. These will not be major supply points with enough materiel to sustain a lengthy campaign. Rather, they may contain one-two DOS to serve both as a reservoir from which maneuver forces can draw when resupply from the seabase is interrupted (e.g., weather) and/or to reduce the demand for aircraft to travel an extended distance to the sea-base. It will also serve as an immediate reserve capability to support any disparities between the flow of supplies from the Fleet and the tactical demand for supplies by the operating forces.

The characteristics of Marine Corps logistics under Expeditionary Force 21 should evolve to be fully capable of:

- Focusing on organizational changes to logistics enablers to support and sustain these dispersed, disaggregated, and afloat forces.
- Being integrated with naval logistics while being interoperable with joint, theater and applicable multi-national logistics capabilities.
- In conjunction with the Navy, expanding access in support of force deployment and sustainment.
- Maximizing MAGTF sustainment from the seabase.
- Forward-deploying select combat engineering capabilities to support the distributed global force presence of SPMAGTFs to include championing naval construction engineering capabilities.
- Supporting the Expeditionary Force 21 global laydown of forward-deployed forces with improved logistics responsiveness and agility while sustaining equipment readiness of disaggregated units.
- Maximizing MAGTF sustainment from the seabase by continued resourcing and integration of key initiatives with the Navy such as cargo routing, material expediting, repairable retrograde, and afloat inventory positioning.
- Supporting a medical common operating picture allowing for smooth transfer of patients advanced care modules and telemedicine links to greatly improve battlefield treatment and evacuation while sharing information directly from the Corpsmen to CRTS.
- Developing a resource plan to expand the expeditionary aviation maintenance capabilities found in the T-AVB vessel with a capacity for ground maintenance support that would also enhance support for Phase 0 and I Theater Security missions.
- Employing more efficient electrical generation and distribution systems, leveraging ground renewable expeditionary energy systems (GREENS) to maximum extent possible.

- Resourcing and maintaining our Bases and Stations to support TECOM Live, Virtual, and Constructive training ranges to support larger number of smaller deploying MAGTFs.

"We must train as we would fight" will also apply to logistics across the MAGTF. Our logistics will be <u>guided</u> by two operating principles in training and when employed:

Support an Expeditionary Mindset

- Task-organized forces ashore, minimal footprint (both personnel and equipment).
- All MAGTF units should evaluate Type I Allowances in their Tables of Equipment (T/E) as to what is truly mission-essential, deployable, expeditionary, and thus...mandatory.
- Bring what you need; live lean in the field (two-man tents).
- To improve mobility and to lighten units, divest quadruple containers (Quadcons) from unit allowances and introduce more expeditionary packaging such as Joint Modular Intermodal Containers (JMICs) across the MAGTFs.
- Live expeditionary and hard ashore, leave creature comforts at sea.
- Request only the resources that directly contribute to mission execution.
- Limit HN infrastructure use unless otherwise directed.
- Plan constantly with the Navy for support from the sea.

Maximize organic capabilities / limit contracting

- Use organic means to make water—train to it; Light Water Purification System-Expanded Capacity Module (LWPS-ECM) and Tactical Water Purification System (TWPS.)
- Generate electricity using both conventional and renewable organic equipment.
- Sustain the force with Meals Ready to Eat (MREs) and Unitized Group Rations (UGRs); No contracted messing.
- Employ HN support as a last resort unless directed by the Embassy.
- Limit contracting to resources not inherent in the MAGTF.

Finally, future operations—just as today—will involve all aspects of the joint force. While we readily focus on logistics support at the tactical level, there are supporting joint logistics actions underway by the U. S. Transportation Command (USTC) and the Defense Logistics Agency (DLA) globally across the strategic and operational (theater) levels of logistics. To assist in planning for future operations, the Marine Corps is a full participant in all joint logistics developments—aligning both NLI and other Marine Corps processes and technologies to take advantage of the synergies that will result from the myriad of joint and allied initiatives and capabilities.

j. Expeditionary Operations. Expeditionary Force 21 envisions a Marine Corps that assures littoral access to enable the naval and joint forces to engage, respond to crisis, and project power. These required activities and operations include creating the conditions for host nations to allow forces to use facilities, establish basing of forces in a potential crisis area, and seizing access when necessary through forcible entry operations. The development of capabilities for expeditionary operations under the Expeditionary Force 21 concept should consider the following dimensions:

- **Diplomatic Access:** requires implementation of forward engagement policy specifically focusing on increased planning, coordination and information exchange with regional MARFORs, Geographic Combatant Commanders, State Department, TSOCs, allies, other partners, and local governments.

- **Geographic Access**: Requires improved connectors with greater range, capacity, and speed and better landing profiles to include at-sea discharge and other craft to provide improved access to littoral inland waterways. Presently, access is limited to boats for littoral maneuver and riverine. Additionally, the LCAC has limited access to 70% of displacement-craft-surveyed beaches, severely limiting access.

- **Military Access**: requires resourcing, fielding, experimentation, exercises, integration and doctrine development for counter-guided rocket, artillery, mortars, and missiles (G-RAMM) capabilities and CONOPS with emphasis on the integration of Blue and Green capabilities approaching and operating within the littorals. This includes UAV, F-35B, AH-1, and small craft considerations. Also includes resurgent support for low-cost naval surface fires improvements to range and precision.

Land-based and sea-based prepositioning must be maintained as a key enabler to access and crisis response. Other considerations include the ability to:

- Rapidly seize, establish, sustain, and protect austere expeditionary bases to enhance the ability of the fleet to operate in A2/AD threat environments.
- Employ new mobile forward arming and refueling points (FARPs) that are rapidly re-locatable and operate as a network to support dispersed F-35B operations.
- Seize lodgment for follow-on joint operations.
- Establish mobile and distributed air and missile defense capabilities to support integrated fire control counter-G-RAMM and area denial defense systems.
- Develop initial assault / raid capability for surface and vertical assault from greater than 65 nm.
- Retain initial 2 x MEB forcible entry capabilities. Each MEB to insert at least 1 battalion landing team (BLT) via single-wave, surface assault and up to 2 BLTs via vertical assault during one period of darkness from 30-50 nm. Follow on surface / ground tactical maneuver capabilities can be deployed via surface and air connectors as required for sustained operations ashore. These capabilities may deploy from MPS or alternative shipping to offset mobility deficiencies within the compositing force.
- Ensure the capability to conduct at-sea transfer of MPS from 30-100 nm from shore with the capability then to maneuver to the shore.
- Conduct experiments and exercises to leverage MSC shipping – to include the MLP, the INLS, and the RRDF, and the JHSV.
- Retain sufficient and compatible follow-on echelon shipping.
- Improve the ability to embark, support, and quickly deploy USMC/NECC/SOF small craft from amphibious shipping or alternative shipping.
- Expeditionary contracting to support steady-state activities, crisis response and power-projection operations.

k. Seabasing. Seabasing incorporates the traditional naval missions of sea control, assuring access, and power projection with an increased emphasis on maneuver from the sea. By expanding access and reducing dependence on land bases, seabasing supports national global strategic objectives and provides needed operational flexibility in an uncertain world. Through seabasing we can establish expeditionary bases at sea in support of GCC requirements. Meeting these requirements and the needs of the Nation necessitate more than the 38 amphibious ship requirement. It requires an integrated naval approach to seabasing that employs warships, alternative shipping and land basing in a complementary manner. Increased steady-state demand and crisis response seabasing requirements must be met through creative integration of all platforms and formations. Complementary MSC alternatives provide options for afloat staging, steady state engagement, crisis response and reinforcement for major combat operations. Key considerations are platforms with C2, medical, aviation, and surface delivery to support a variety of mission profiles.

There are immediate and near-term options available to provide MAGTFs with a degree of vertical and surface naval expeditionary capability via a combination of traditional and alternative afloat platforms. For example, MAGTFs currently positioned geographically with MV-22s could be embarked on a combination of LMSRs, T-AKEs and a single deployer amphibious ship acting as a 'mothership'.

JHSVs are capable of carrying 600 short tons of cargo and supplies and supporting 104 troops for a total of 14 days without replenishment. JHSVs are certified to operate with CH-53 and smaller aircraft. While the JHSVs can handle the weight of the MV-22 aircraft, flight deck thermal management (deck heating) issues must be addressed and resolved. At this time, JHSVs are capable of conducting vertical replenishment operations with MV-22s.

The MPF Dry Cargo and Ammunition Ships (T-AKEs) can support approximately 100 troops for indefinite periods. T-AKEs are certified to operate with MV-22s, thereby coupling the T-AKE's supply support selective offload capabilities with the MV-22's operational reach. T-AKEs have excellent planning spaces, commercial broad-band satellite capabilities, and secret internet protocol network (SIPRNET) connections.

The MPF LMSR ships can accommodate approximately 100 troops for indefinite periods of time. While the LMSRs do not have the communications and planning space capabilities of the T-AKEs, those ships do carry significant amounts of wheeled vehicles, tanks, and heavy equipment, which will become accessible at-sea upon the delivery of the MLP. Innovative uses of the C4ISR equipment embarked in the holds of those ships and C2 augmentation from a joint communications support element (or like equipment) could offset the lack of organic LMSR communications and planning capabilities and give force commanders yet another option for force deployment and employment.

Each Maritime Prepositioning Ship squadron will have one MLP as those ships begin entering service in FY15. Effectively a 'pier in the ocean', the MLP will be capable of conducting at-sea, sea state-3 skin-to-skin marriage with LMSRs, receiving equipment and supplies from the LMSRs (up to and including M1A1 tanks), and transferring those stocks to LCACs that are landed on the MLP. The MLP does not possess any designed troop berthing (approximately 20 surge berths may be available). Its 25K square foot raised vehicle deck is open to the weather, and the MLP is not currently designed to husband and maintain LCACs. MLPs are, however, designed to accommodate troop berthing modules supporting up to approximately 400 personnel. Such modules are not currently planned or programmed for MLP integration. A more detailed evaluation of how messing, food storage, shower, waste, and other systems would need to be conducted to determine how this surge in personnel would impact services. Additional MLPs are being designed as afloat staging bases, and these vessels could provide near-term solutions to support steady-state and crisis operations in AFRICOM and PACOM when integrated with a MAGTF and regionally oriented MEB.

Given the capabilities of the JHSV, T-AKE, LMSR, and MLP noted above, and with the addition of a single amphibious ship (LPD or LSD) to act as a mother ship for troops, aircraft, landing craft, and the like, these platforms taken together could provide crisis response MAGTFs significant dispersed littoral maneuver capabilities -- both vertical and surface with significant sustainment support -- to meet a wide range of combatant commander missions short of Joint Forcible Entry Operations. Seabasing in Expeditionary Force 21 will be characterized by the capability to:

- Ensure sufficient shipping to meet steady-state operations, crisis response and power projection demand from combatant commanders.
- Aggregate globally distributed naval forces into tailored force packages.
- Deploy/employ SPMAGTF, MEU and MEB-sized forces via amphibious and maritime pre-positioning shipping.
- Provide sufficient, compatible assault follow-on echelon shipping.
- Indefinitely sustain a MEF conducting operations in the littorals from a seabase.
- Conduct C2 of littoral operations ashore from a seabase.

l. MAGTF-SOF Integration. In order to enhance our ability to execute the assigned tasks outlined in this document, we must seek every opportunity to collaborate, plan, exercise and experiment with Special Operations Forces in order to achieve operational synergy during steady-state, crisis response and contingency operations. As USSOCOM and the TSOCs seek to persistently position SOF in key potential partner and crisis areas, expeditionary MAGTFs could potentially leverage information SOF has garnered during normal preparation activities. Additionally we need to explore further integration into the TSOCs in the form of permanent staff or liaison. Further integration with TSOCs will significantly contribute to operational awareness and effectiveness for the MAGTF. Considerations include:

- Deliberate and early integration of SOF planners in major USMC exercises.
- Deliberate and early integration of SOF planners for service War games.
- Development of limited objective experiments focused on operational and capabilities integration in complex terrain and circumstances that explore relationships, information sharing and equipment interoperability.
- Deliberate planning opportunities between the regional MARFOR, NAVFOR and TSOC for security cooperation events.

m. High Quality People – The Foundation of Marine Corps Readiness. The operational innovations inherent in Expeditionary Force 21 will be enabled by, and stand upon, the bedrock of our Corps: the individual Marine. Marines are forged in hard training, made wise through years of combat, and imbued with an expeditionary mindset. We live hard, thrive in austerity, and embrace innovation. This expeditionary ethos and the extraordinary warriors who exemplify it have and always will be the foundation of our Corps. Our investment in Marines as the cornerstone of all other capabilities will be characterized by two enduring and interrelated lines of effort:

Maintaining the Highest Levels of Combat Readiness. We will capitalize upon every opportunity to enhance Marines' warfighting capabilities and the ability to operate in a joint and coalition environment. The agile Marine Corps of Expeditionary Force 21 will require sustained investments in preparing Marines as the key contributor to the readiness of our deployed, ready to deploy, and supporting organizations. Considerations include:

- Manpower policies and processes that collectively support the readiness of standard and task-organized forces of the Active and Reserve Components.
- A 'cohesion' mindset that fosters engaged, focused leadership at all levels.

- Continuing our commitment to attract, mentor and retain the best and brightest of America's sons and daughters.
- An effectively managed civilian workforce, tied to readiness, and which ensures the Marine Corps remains ready to respond to tomorrow's crises with today's forces.

Keeping Faith with Marines and Families. In order to support the attributes of Expeditionary Force 21, the Marine Corps will remain committed to providing Marines and their families with a comprehensive and effective support system, as readiness on the home-front ensures mission readiness. The Marine Corps is committed to the Marine during their entire lifecycle through separation or retirement and beyond. As the Marine Corps returns to an expeditionary force, we are working to increase the strength of protective factors, including healthy relationships among our Marines and their families. Nurturing the resiliency of families and children ultimately supports the readiness of Marines and is a priority of the Marine Corps. Keeping faith with Marines and families in Expeditionary Force 21 will be characterized by the capability to:

- Ensure that our Marines and families are fully aware of the various resources and programs available to them and that they are encouraged to make use of these resources.
- Provide comprehensive Marine and family programs to develop totally fit Marines and families who are resilient in all areas of life (to include the physical, psychological, social, and spiritual dimensions) and engage in healthy behaviors that enable them to successfully meet their duties while deployed and in garrison.
- Provide Marine and family programs that use evidence-based practices.
- Ensure all Marine and family programs meet all credentialing and accreditation to ensure consistency of care across the Marine Corps.
- Continually assess programs to ensure access and availability of care and support across all installations, to reservists, and those supporting the reserve component throughout the country.
- Provide Marine and family programs that are flexible enough to surge and retract as necessary to support the demands of future missions or training requirements.
- Provide safe havens aboard our bases and stations that promote healthy communities, and provide valued Marine, family, and community support programs and services.
- Remain wholly committed to our wounded, ill, and injured Marines, Sailors and their families as we assist them in their transition back to duty or to civilian life.

4. Conclusion.

Within the implementation are multiple goals, challenges and objectives which are meant to push the Marine Corps forward. The document is aspirational and all of these will not be immediately achieved; rather they provide the target for force development. These goals will be assessed annually.

"We are, by our nature, 'expeditionary.' This means several things. It means a high state of readiness; we can go at a moment's notice. It means our organization, our equipment, our structure are designed to allow us to deploy very efficiently...It's a mind-set, too, about being ready to go, about being ready to be deployed, and about flexibility. We can easily and quickly move from fighting to humanitarian operations."

*- **General Tony Zinni, USMC***
Battle Ready, 2004